Bible
Interpretations
Twenty Second Series
October 4 – December 27, 1896

I Kings, II Corinthians, Proverbs & Ecclesiastes

Bible
Interpretations
Twenty-second Series

I Kings, II Corinthians, Proverbs & Ecclesiastes

These Bible Interpretations were published in the Inter-Ocean Newspaper in Chicago, Illinois during the late eighteen nineties.

By
Emma Curtis Hopkins

President of the Emma Curtis Hopkins Theological Seminary at Chicago, Illinois

WISEWOMAN PRESS

Bible Interpretations: Twenty-second Series

By Emma Curtis Hopkins

© WiseWoman Press 2014

Managing Editor: Michael Terranova

ISBN: 978-0945385-73-8

WiseWoman Press

Vancouver, WA 98665

www.wisewomanpress.com

www.emmacurtishopkins.com

CONTENTS

Editors Note

All lessons starting with the Seventh Series of Bible Interpretations will be Sunday postings from the Inter-Ocean Newspaper in Chicago, Illinois. Many of the lessons in the following series were retrieved from the International New Thought Association Archives, in Mesa, Arizona by, Rev Joanna Rogers. Many others were retrieved from libraries in Chicago, and the Library of Congress, by Rev. Natalie Jean.

All the lessons follow the Sunday School Lesson Plan published in "Peloubet's International Sunday School Lessons". The passages to be studied are selected by an International Committee of traditional Bible Scholars.

Some of the Emma's lessons don't have a title. In these cases the heading will say "Comments and Explanations of the Golden Text," followed by the Bible passages to be studied.

Foreword

By Rev. Natalie R. Jean

I have read many teachings by Emma Curtis Hopkins, but the teachings that touch the very essence of my soul are her Bible Interpretations. There are many books written on the teachings of the Bible, but none can touch the surface of the true messages more than these Bible interpretations. With each word you can feel and see how Spirit spoke through Emma. The mystical interpretations take you on a wonderful journey to Self Realization.

Each passage opens your consciousness to a new awareness of the realities of life. The illusions of life seem to disappear through each interpretation. Emma teaches that we are the key that unlocks the doorway to the light that shines within. She incorporates ideals of other religions into her teachings, in order to understand the commonalities, so that there is a complete understanding of our Oneness. Emma opens our eyes and mind to a better today and exciting future.

Emma Curtis Hopkins, one of the Founders of New Thought teaches us to love ourselves, to speak our Truth, and to focus on our Good. My life has moved in wonderful directions because of her teachings. I know the only thing that can move me in this world is God. May these interpretations guide you to a similar path and may you truly remember that "There Is Good For You and You Ought to Have It."

Introduction

Emma Curtis Hopkins was born in 1849 in Killingsly, Connecticut. She passed on April 8, 1925. Mrs. Hopkins had a marvelous education and could read many of the worlds classical texts in their original language. During her extensive studies she was always able to discover the Universal Truths in each of the world's sacred traditions. She quotes from many of these teachings in her writings. As she was a very private person, we know little about her personal life. What we do know has been gleaned from other people or from the archived writings we have been able to discover.

Emma Curtis Hopkins was one of the greatest influences on the New Thought movement in the United States. She taught over 50,000 people the Universal Truth of knowing "God is All there is." She taught many of founders of early New Thought, and in turn these individuals expanded the influence of her teachings. All of her writings encourage the student to enter into a personal relationship with God. She presses us to deny anything except the Truth of this spiritual Presence in every area of our lives. This is the central focus of all her teachings.

The first six series of Bible Interpretations were presented at her seminary in Chicago, Illinois. The remaining Series', probably close to thirty, were printed in the Inter Ocean Newspaper in Chicago. Many of the lessons are no longer available for various reasons. It is the intention of WiseWoman Press to publish as many of these Bible Interpretations as possible. Our hope is that any missing lessons will be found or directed to us.

I am very honored to join the long line of people that have been involved in publishing Emma Curtis Hopkins's Bible Interpretations. Some confusion exists as to the numbering sequence of the lessons. In the early 1920's many of the lessons were published by the Highwatch Fellowship. Inadvertently the first two lessons were omitted from the numbering system. Rev. Joanna Rogers has corrected this mistake by finding the first two lessons and restoring them to their rightful place in the order. Rev. Rogers has been able to find many of the missing lessons at the International New Thought Alliance archives in Mesa, Arizona. Rev. Rogers painstakingly scoured the archives for the missing lessons as well as for Mrs. Hopkins other works. She has published much of what was discovered. WiseWoman Press is now publishing the correctly numbered series of the Bible Interpretations.

In the early 1940's, there was a resurgence of interest in Emma's works. At that time, Highwatch Fellowship began to publish many of her writings, and it was then that *High Mysticism*, her seminal work was published. Previously, the material contained in High Mysticism was only available as individual lessons and was brought together in book form for the first time. Although there were many errors in these first publications and many Bible verses were incorrectly quoted, I am happy to announce that WiseWoman Press is now publishing *High Mysticism* in the a corrected format. This corrected form was scanned faithfully from the original, individual lessons.

The next person to publish some of the Bible Lessons was Rev. Marge Flotron from the Ministry of Truth International in Chicago, Illinois. She published the Bible Lessons as well as many of Emma's other works. By her initiative, Emma's writings were brought to a larger audience when DeVorss & Company, a longtime publisher of Truth Teachings, took on the publication of her key works.

In addition, Dr. Carmelita Trowbridge, founding minister of The Sanctuary of Truth in Alhambra, California, inspired her assistant minister, Rev. Shirley Lawrence, to publish many of Emma's works, including the first three series of Bible Interpretations. Rev. Lawrence created mail order courses for many of these Series. She has graciously passed on any information she had, in order to assure that these works continue to inspire individuals and groups who are called to further study of the teachings of Mrs. Hopkins.

Finally, a very special acknowledgement goes to Rev Natalie Jean, who has worked diligently to retrieve several of Emma's lessons from the Library of Congress, as well as libraries in Chicago. Rev. Jean hand-typed many of the lessons she found on microfilm. Much of what she found is on her website, www.highwatch.net.

It is with a grateful heart that I am able to pass on these wonderful teachings. I have been studying dear Emma's works for fifteen years. I was introduced to her writings by my mentor and teacher, Rev. Marcia Sutton. I have been overjoyed with the results of delving deeply into these Truth Teachings.

In 2004, I wrote a Sacred Covenant entitled "Resurrecting Emma," and created a website, www.emmacurtishopkins.com. The result of creating this covenant and website has brought many of Emma's works into my hands and has deepened my faith in God. As a result of my love for these works, I was led to become a member of Wise-Woman Press and to publish these wonderful teachings. God is Good.

My understanding of Truth from these divinely inspired teachings keeps bringing great Joy, Freedom, and Peace to my life.

Dear reader; It is with an open heart that I offer these works to you, and I know they will touch you as they have touched me. Together we are living in the Truth that God is truly present, and living for and through each of us.

The greatest Truth Emma presented to us is "My Good is my God, Omnipresent, Omnipotent and Omniscient."

Rev. Michael Terranova

WiseWoman Press

Vancouver, Washington, 2010

LESSON I

A Study In The Science Of The Lightning

I Kings 1

This lesson might be called "A Study in the Science of the Lightning," for it tells of the instantaneous. The man who by any stroke of luck or correct formula shall find out exactly what Jesus Christ meant by his life and works shall have the science of the lightning. "For as the lightning cometh out of the east and shineth, even unto the west; so shall also the coming of the son of man be." (Matt, 24:27) "The son of man," as we all know, means all the people exposed as superhuman.

Commencing with the first July lesson, all the selections are said to be practically intended to relate to governments, as empires, republics, kingdoms. They have heretofore been using David of Israel as an object lesson. Now they are to use Solomon as an object lesson. David came in from

1

the people. He represented the history of any nation which purports to be: governed by and for the people. He has been pictured sometimes by the lessons in a fashion to show how it is with nations where the people at large have little or no voice in affairs.

Solomon comes in on a King's line, he is not to represent the people, but he is to handle them kindly and judiciously. They are to be kept in constant awe and admiration of the piles of gold he represents and the gorgeous apparel he can wear, by reason of the prosperity secured to the throne of David, this Solomon is to outshine in carriages, jewelry, and wardrobes all the other kings, queens, lords, and princes of the whole world.

His mother was Bathsheba, renowned for her beauty. His father was King David, renowned for his valor and majesty. His clothes, purchased by the prosperity David got while true to the people's interests, are to set the fashions for foreign courts. His harems are to teach foreign kings points they have never dreamed of in the way of destroying remembrances of what home means. His career as a father of kings to come is to end by his son, Rehoboam, who has been called an idiot by some excited historians. For Rehoboam, who was the only offspring Solomon could manage to secure from his 700 wives, had the kingdom wrenched away from him as related in First Kings, twelfth chapter.

This Solomon, with all the wealth of nations at his command, with all the education of schools and state at his tongue's end, with the adoration of a whole globe glorifying him, is to be one step only removed from the revolt. He shall flourish very well for a season, then his personal habits shall get the better of him, and, suddenly, in Rehoboam, shall his kingships in material splendor end. After 1,000 years it shall rise again in Jesus, King by his mysterious taste of God.

The section chosen for today does not look ahead so far and prophesy for coming history, but relates to the sudden and unexpected enthronement of Solomon, the pleasure of the high dignitaries in his ascension, and the terror of

Adonijah, who had been hoping that his cheaper crowd of adjuncts might sweep himself through the throne by their enthusiasm over the coup d'etat. — First chapter, I Kings.

The lesson, as it relates imperatively to the present state of affairs in some measure in every government on earth, is to be found in I Kings, first chapter. It tells plainly that the David kind of rule now practically ends, for the majority of the people have already made up their minds to vote for Solomon. They cannot realize it, however, for David is still in sight though decrepit. It seems to them that Solomon will do even better by them than David has done. It is David's choice that Solomon, his golden-charioted son, his court-bred son, shall reign, and the multitude shout gleefully, not seeing Rehoboam ahead, when David commands them to shout.

Read over the whole first chapter of I Kings. It relates to this day. If you do not see Rehoboam ahead you will belong exclusively to the present hilarious confidence. If you do see Rehoboam ahead you will have to fix your eyes on the hidden wires that are pulling in the real lover of the world this way. You will have to fix them hard on the lover of men whose face does not exhibit itself in the flesh very vividly just now, except to the watchers on Zion's top. You will have to be a watcher on Zion if you want to keep your eyes from seeing the modern Solomon's paw.

Solomon is crowned suddenly and unexpectedly. While the nation is expecting a change of government, and largely supposing that Jeroboam is coming along, lo! Solomon is suddenly set on the throne. The main influence of the chapter is the feeling of suddenness it gives. Now, this feeling of suddenness is meant to be the hint to more than it mentions in the chapter. It is meant to amputate our idea of tedious slowness in all that pertains to goodness. It is, as we all see, the settled idea of a whole world that it takes good events a long time to arrive. This lessons digs out and cuts off that idea. It hurries along the worldly wise Solomon. It declares that Rehoboam's reign will be almost nothing. It skips over the centuries and brings Jesus Christ to the throne. And in him shall all the nations of the earth be blest. There shall be war no more. They shall hunger no more. They shall weep no more. They shall not compete any more. Each one shall know his own place and be glad to keep it.

The forty-eighth verse is the one that hurries in the face of Jesus Christ on the throne. It is the secret golden text. Read how swift it is. "Blessed be the Lord God of Israel, which hath given One to sit on my throne this day, mine eyes even seeing it."

"In that day there shall be one Lord and his name One." David fixed his eyes on Solomon, a lad of 20, but he was speaking the mystic name of the Almighty One. Therefore he made a delay. It is the purpose of this chapter to hint strongly to us to fix our eyes somewhere else than on candidates for kingly chairs, and call some other name than any kingly candidate now confidently struggling in the race for a chair. For this other way of looking, and this name, are the only swift-lightning plan ever offered to man.

This lesson, read with the knowledge that its influence is swiftness and its golden text says "now," will cause a kind of surgery we have never yet experienced to take place. Just think of seeing the joy of our eyes, the glad friend of our world and ourself, this day! Not tomorrow, but today! Will not this amputate our idea of time? The Bible is full of hints of a science capable of eliminating time, as if time were the ugly veil hanging be-

tween the splendors of Paradise and our eager
eyes.

"Her days shall not be prolonged.
   My word shall not be prolonged any more.
And sware that there should be time no longer.
   There came a great voice, saying, "it is done."
While they are yet speaking I will hear.
   Before they can call I will answer.
Even so, come quickly, Lord Jesus."

It is beginning to be found out that the prophecies of the Bible have been not only spiritually but
literally carried out so far as they are already finished. Take the prophecies of Daniel for example.
All that the man told Daniel in chapters 10, 11,
and 12 has taken place except the Michael and the
stone part. The last king mentioned as being finally driven into planting his temporary throne in
Jerusalem, verse 45, is the present Sultan of Turkey. By his external, material conduct he is
representing the present attitude of mankind toward the unsuccessful and the helpless. He not
only stands and massacres the Armenians to suit
himself, but he externalizes the feelings of the
sensuously prospered of every nation now on earth
toward all the under dogs in the fight of life. And
the day he falls this literal representative of our
merchant princes, our presidents, our kings, our
czars our emperors, that day standeth up Michael,
the great prince that standeth for my people. In
the secret hearts of many Michael is even now

standing up, but one day a literal Michael shall rise with splendid strength for my people.

All that transpires outwardly has first to take place in 'the strength of the sentiments, or hearts, or spirit.

'What the spirit promises
    Nature will perform."

There is a strong sentiment stirring now to inquire why some are always kept down and kept under who are carrying out their natures and doing their parts, while others are raised up and praised who do no better. It is beginning to be seen as the result of some principle promulgated by somebody and believed in by many. Somebody spoke of the divine right of kings to rule as they pleased. Thousands caught at the saying. So now every kingdom is heavily taxed to support the pomp of its king or queen. This statement started in a truth of the throne place located in all men alike, but was accepted narrowly. Whoever can manage to scramble back onto his own throne will find the whole world obeying his orders, as last Sunday's lesson showed. And if every man, woman, child on this earth sits on his own throne place he will collide with nobody and tax nobody. It is the conscious recollection of our birth in God and not in matter. It was the message of Jesus Christ: "Call no man upon earth your father, for one is your father, even God."

7

Today's lesson is meant to hurry us on to our throne place, where we can see today just what country is lying around us and who are its inhabitants. "One sits on my throne this day, mine eyes even seeing it." (Verse 48)

This lesson might be called the redeemed pledge, for it is the literal fulfillment of David's pledge to Bathsheba. This widow of Uriah, whose name was Bathsheba, represents life in the body of flesh everywhere — the people who depend on their brains and bodies. They are doing as well as they know how. They eat, drink, sleep, study, fight, marry, keep house, print newspapers, run street cars, compete with each other for money, high chairs, yellow jackets, yellow crowns,, etc. And to the scrambling lot a promise, a pledge, has been given that one day something wonderfully good, divinely kind, shall come. How long this scrambling lot feels that it has been kept out of the fulfillment of that pledge?

They shall not hurt nor kill in all my holy mountain. They shall hunger no more, neither for bread nor for strength. They shall run and not be weary. They shall restore themselves to the beauty of God as they first had it in the days when they had never faced flesh; when the ravishing light of eternity's suns kissed the singing mountains of heaven, where they lived; when the voices of their world sounded sweet on their ears everywhere, so sweet that there was no doubt in their hearts about the omnipotence of goodness and wisdom.

It is said that when the curtain of time was hung up this scrambling set forgot about the country they hailed from and sang about it as a country to come. They raised up priests to preach about a future time, when the veil of time should be torn away. They raised up bards to sing of some one to come who should tear it off, as he will destroy the veil spread over the nations. And this lesson says, too, that one whom the scrambling crew have called "Lord God" shall suddenly — today — show us the throne. (Verse 48) Then the Bible is full of the proclamation that Jesus of Nazareth is this Lord God tearing off now, today, this veil of time, and it intimates that David, causing Bathsheba to see her son placed on the throne just exactly as he had pledged unto her, is the world seeing today suddenly, exactly what its prophets, priests, and bards have pledged to it.

It proclaims that all that takes place now shall take place quickly. It shows how rapidly the coming earthly magnates will show up their Solomon natures, how swiftly they will drop into their Rehoboam senilities, how speedily all their doings will run over the thousand circles between Rehoboam, who could do nothing, and Jesus, who could do everything.

Taking this lesson individually there can be no doubt but what each one will now see the fulfillment of some good prognostication once made to and for him. Let him look out for it now. Let him take hold upon it today. This lesson asks us to accept forgiveness for time as though it were something we ourselves were to blame for. It tells that every time we see a promise kept we have been forgiven for time in some way. It tells us to be utterly forgiven for time by having time utterly swept away.

There is something here this instant. It has always been here, and it will always be here. It has been pledged to us as though it were something to come, to be manufactured for us, but this way of pledging is a ruse of the very time itself to keep itself going. The wonderful something is here now — "This day, mine eyes even seeing it." — (Verse 48)

That which, tears away the veil of time is a power with a name. Its throne is within ourselves. It is not compassed around by the flesh. There is no room for him in the inn of flesh, they said in Jerusalem. It is not compassed around by the mind of the brain. There was no mind could contain all that he signified in Jerusalem. "Yet I will make my abode in you," he said, and today the eyes see that it is so.

The only science worth while is the science of the lightning. Except a man see today the end of his pledges he is not in with the science of the lightning. David was old. The prognostications are now all old. Solomon was new and sudden, though he had been on hand for nineteen years. Bathsheba was frightened and childish. So, now, with our world, the greater than Solomon, has been here 1,900 years, but his enthronement is sudden and new to a frightened and childish world.

So, now, let us hush our crying, for today is some wonderful fulfillment of hope coming to each one of us. It is the direct hand of the living God on the helm of our life. Let us shout for the city is ours. Let us sing, for our warfare is ended.

Inter Ocean-Newspaper, October 4, 1896

LESSON II

Solomon's Wise Choice

1 Kings, Chapter 3

The subject of this lesson is, "Solomon's Wise Choice." What was his choice? To govern Israel with an able hand; to have great understanding of people's minds; to have uncommon shrewdness in manipulating them; to know all about trees, plants, stones, insects, stars, and statesmanship. Did he succeed? He did. Of the plants he understood all, "from the cedars of Lebanon to the hyssop that springeth on the wall." Of the people's minds he had such understanding that he drew forth perpetual gasps of awe and admiration from them. Of the mysteries of stones and states he had such understanding that the great Queen of Sheba conceded that he surpassed all other men. She tried him by deep devices common to those times and he never failed to astonish her with his wits.

She sent to his court 1,000 slaves some of the men slaves dressed in woman's clothes, and some of the women slaves dressed in men's clothes. He knew the men from the women at once; by the way they washed their faces.

She sent the query by post to him, as to how an unperforated pearl should be pierced. He perforated one immediately by the use of an occult stone he had discovered.

She queried how an intricately pierced diamond should be strung. He inserted a small worm into the diamond. The worm wound its way through and left a silk thread behind, so that Solomon sent the diamond to the Queen, strung on a thread of impossible manufacture.

She asked how a goblet could be filled with water which had come neither from the clouds nor the earth. He caught the sweat from a fiery young horse and filled the goblet full.

She asked what it is that comes from the dust; whose food is dust; can be poured out like water, and illuminate a house. He said that naptha answered the description. Oh, how shrewd he was in all that wisdom he had asked to have! (I Kings 5:8-15)

The chief hint in this lesson is not, however, the success of Solomon in getting his prayers answered, though he certainly stands on record as one of the most competent prayers of history; no, that chief hint is contained within his words: "I am but a little child." Today's light beams on the head of somebody whose experience with this wonderful world has ended, though they yet walk upon it.

And that one has begun the heavenly dispensation, here and now, dwelling among us in the flesh, but shedding abroad the influence of the heavenly fire that glows through him — or her. This one indeed has become a little child. The sweetest theme of Jesus Christ was, "Except ye become as little children ye cannot see the kingdom of God."

Now to become a little child is to repent — to turn back — to turn back — retrace the steps of the mind. Back — back, let the mind return — back to the heavenly bosom whence it sprang. Back to the glad stillness out of whose balmy ecstasy the songs of the morning stars arose before ever their dusty wheels let fall the asteroids of space. The journey is not long, though the books of man have whispered of eons on eons since the children of time came journeying away from that bosom of peace. Back — back, let the mind turn, back to its home in the beautiful garden, where the tunes of the nightingales first started forth. The beautiful garden where childhood is inspired by intelligent consciousness, and needs nothing, for it knows itself and its powers. The journey is not hard though the books of the world have declared that it is a rough and thorny way back to our home; though they have told how steep is the hill between us and there, how deep and black is the river, how dark is the night. Today's lesson takes Solomon, a man grown, a married, world-taught adult, and shows how by one glance of his words into the unwordable facts of our being, he caught at the horns of humanity's dilemma and shook the beast of ignorance, inferiority, shame, and defeat till it gave down its secrets concerning this world and the ways of beating it on its own lines.

First, let us make note that Solomon saw all this in a dream, which signifies that all that he was talking about and talking to was unreality. He talked to the prince of this world, he talked of the men of this world, he shook the whole fabric of nature with the vehemence of his human mind to make it give him skill sufficient to get and keep the awe and obedience of the multitudes; not their recognition of their equality with him as divinely born sons and daughters of the everlasting King of Kings.

Let us make careful note here. That Lord and that skill he addressed were dreams, unreality the mortal shadow, the symbol only, of the real fact. He said in words: "I am but a little child." His words were truth. But whosoever is dealing with words of truth is in the realm of the dream. In the realm of the awake they do not tell the truth by words to anybody. For to whom should they tell the truth, since all know it equally well?

Jesus was explicit on this point of all mankind knowing equally well with himself and having equal power with himself. Solomon was explicit on the point of himself being the one to govern other men, to show off before other men, to keep ahead of other men. Therefore Jesus, when speaking of the difference between Solomon's attitude of mind and all other men's attitudes of mind said Solomon's was ahead because he dealt first hand with the principles of nature. He talked with abstract nature itself, he married his mind to all the secrets of the mind and energy of nature. Thus he got his ascendancy by the God power of nature. He struck its chords by words of truth. He caught the mystery of mastering men, animals, and mechanics by intellectual enchantment. In other words, he caught the occult. This is as high as any Oriental ever gets. It is the Solomon of agility of mind, the Solomon of strength of mind, the Solomon wisdom.

But Jesus Christ said that in Him was a greater than Solomon. Then He explained why. Because He sought not to govern or instruct men as His kingly role, but to identify Himself with the undescribed Almighty One of whom the occult power is but a symbol. He would touch the Almighty One and by his touch be glorified with childhood as it is in the bosom of the Divine One. And by his touch all mankind should be glorified with actual childhood as it is in the splendor and majesty of him where all are free and none obey, where all are equal and none rule. "That where I am ye may be also."

He showed that Solomon sought earthly secrets as they are found in the realm of the occult before their actions are sprung before the helpless gaze of mankind. Solomon by shaking the horns of that prince of the world who reigns where he will and only the divinely inspired can prevail against him could maintain 700 wives and 300 concubines, could perforate unpierced pearls, and string fine diamonds; he won the admiration of Balkis, beauteous Queen of the South; he built aqueducts, fortresses; he organized and equipped armies; he spread the waters with his navy; he knew all about nature, as it shows its face in men and women, trees, and rocks, in dreams and occult mysteries.

Jesus by addressing the unnamed One above nature, uncognizant of nature, touched a key back of the occult. He knew what he was about when he said: "Seek ye first the kingdom of God, and all these things shall be added unto you." He might have had a million wives but he married himself to the third presence in the universe. He might have astonished the Caesars with his pomp and splendor, but he watched the morning glory on the hills of Paradise instead. He, too, might have strung diamonds and caught the sweat of fiery horses to answer the riddles of queens, but he strung the soul of man to the soul of the Father, he caught the smile of heaven, with its mansions of rest, instead, mansions for all of us — even the cheapest of us. The divinity of unalterable innocent childhood in the silliest and wickedest of us. He chose that way of dealing with the same Israelites whom Solomon prayed, so skillfully to subdue.

There is myself as I appear. There is all that faces me. These are both but signs and flags thrown out. As Carlyle1 discovered, "All physical things are emblems." There is, however, something actual. It is not an emblem. It is above, beneath, around us. The powers, intelligences, energies, beauties of nature, even to the occult springs of which the Orientals drink, are all fine emblems, but the third presence is not an emblem. It is the heavenly fire which, if a man bathe himself in, he shall never marry 700 wives and flaunt them in the faces of the Czars and Kaisers, the crawling paupers, and the laboring citizens of earth as evidences of his greatness. He shall not seek to govern men. He shall not be alert to propound and answer riddles. He shall not equip an army to defend his country. He shall not build mills and stores to employ his poorer neighbors. He shall not try to eclipse his brethren. He shall not run in the race with any man. Yet he shall be master, king, owner, savior of all that lift dumb cries. He shall draw aside the emblem called nature, whose true name is the prince of the world, and let the smiling divinity go free, exposed. This is the third presence. It is not I as I feel or think. It is not ye who face me in multitudes or singly. It is the Other One whom eye hath not seen nor ear heard; neither hath it entered into our heart to conceive.

With this introduction we will take up the verses of this third chapter of I Kings and render their meanings.

Verse 5, "In Gibeon the Lord appeared to Solomon in a dream by night and God said, Ask what I shall give thee."

"Gibeon" means height. If we speak of physical high places we mention hills and mountains. If we speak of intellectual high places we mention strong ideas which make people stand or sit high up in the estimation of their fellow men. If we speak of divine heights we cannot describe them. Solomon was made a King. This raised his strongest idea to its utmost height. If anybody will take special notice of his strongest idea, if anybody will let every other idea drop but that one, he will be surprised at the feeling of ascension he will feel. An idea can rise when not weighted down by other ideas. Some people call this concentration. Whatever idea gets itself aloof from other ideas till it rises finds itself lording over all other ideas.

Solomon was no exception. His strongest idea concerned itself about excelling everybody and everything. It took his whole mind and body and set them in Gibeon, that is, high up. "Now," says the independent idea, "what shall I do?" Then Solomon proceeded not to ask to be married to the Divine Presence, not to bathe in the heavenly fire whose effect would be to show him the majesty and divinity in all mankind, but to ask for shrewdness in managing men and events.

Verse 6, "And Solomon said, Thou hast showed unto thy servant David, my father, great mercy, and thou hast kept for him this great kindness, that thou hast given him a son to sit on his throne, as it is this day."

There is no doubt but what Solomon supposed, that the energy of the cyclone, the material prowess of kings, the beauty in women was the heighth of godly dealings, that is nature at her unreliable moods of giving to David and withholding from David was God himself. But this energy is only the occult starting point. It is the prince of this world. It is as far from the God of Jesus as the bite of a snake.

Solomon faced the secret heights of nature. That is he faced the mind of the prince of this world. This is not God indeed, though; it is the occult mystery whereby many men got powerful and successful. He spoke of the mercies this force had shown to his father. This very mention of mercy hints at the unmercifulness of the prince of this world. Human nature! Big fishes eating little ones, cats eating birds, the duchess shooting deer*. These are the movements of the prince of this world. We say it is nature. We speak of the cruelty inherent in man; we speak of the kindness inherent in man. We are but speaking of the moods of the prince of this world. He is as high as men get in describing their God: "I make good and create evil. I form the light and create darkness."

Life evermore is fed by death,
    In earth and air and sky,
And that a rose may breathe its breath
    Something must die."

That is the doings of the prince unto whom Solomon was speaking, but not the God unto whom Jesus talked. Solomon was talking with his idea at its point of occult dominion. But it was not the third presence, out of the reach of ideas. He did not get out of ideas.

Jesus let all ideas go and said; "I came not to do mine own will." He had no choice. He had no judgment. In his humiliation his judgment was taken away. But Solomon kept his head level. His idea was his own to the last. He never forgot to want to excel all other men. He praised the prince of this world by telling him how good he had been to let David have a son who could get a higher idea than anybody else concerning governing his neighbors, taxing them high and yet keeping their tongues still. This interpretation of course, will be considered treason to all former renderings of Solomon's dream conversation, but with the candle of Jesus Christ in one hand we are obligated to say it is truth.

Verse 7, "I am but a little child."

Facing his highest idea at its occult lording opportunity he felt its powerfulness. He felt its mystery. He knew that it had a scientific adroitness, splendid strength, sharp acumen to handle his neighbors with. He let it have its own way. Every idea has science to it as every boil has its own run. Fevers act one way; dyspepsias act other ways. Each knows his own run. The same is true of ideas. Let a fever get to going, give it its run, and it is bound to do its work scientifically. Let an idea get to going, give it its run, and it is bound to do its work scientifically.

Verse 8, "Give, therefore, thy servant an understanding heart to judge thy people that I may discern between good and bad."

How great a power it has always been considered to tell good from bad. But to Jesus all men alike came forth from God and were bound to repent or return to God. To him they all seemed God. No evil had any power. No good defended anybody. The Heavenly Third was the fire in which he bathed and forthwith came out seeing paradise everywhere. He that sticks to his own idea till it raises Gibeon high and never drops it, comes back able to discern between good men and bad men.

Solomon became a great judge, a great separator of men from men and women from women. But Jesus picked up the lepers and loved them. He touched the decrepit old women as sacred daughters of the eternal king. He came to fold sinners to his heart with healing breaths of forgetfulness of their humiliating ostracisms. Solomon wanted little children whipped often and much, but Jesus said their faces being turned toward the Heavenly fire their lives were stainless and crimeless. This is treason to the Solomon type of religious exercise, but it is a waft from the body of the young one now in our midst, the child man returned to his home in the infinite bosom of the third presence, not you as you appear best or worst not me as I appear, no, the Heavenly fire — the world's desire.

As this lesson has for its keynote the little child, somebody must be here now on earth — not as a child newly born in its cradle, but as a grown adult with the smile of wisdom and innocence in his face, or her face. You can tell that one if you meet him or her by the speed with which all things stand round and arrange themselves to make harmony, peace, gladness, prosperity, health. Everybody sings. Nobody weeps. Everybody is beautiful. Nobody is hideous. There is a noble equality. There is no judging between the worthy poor and the worthless. This also is treason to the charity Christianity built upon the Solomon plan of dissection.

Verse 10, "And the speech pleased the Lord."

The prince of this world smiles when you shoot partridges successfully. He is pleased if you hunt slaves successfully. He likes you to be successful in cheating. Whatever you do be certain to touch the occult springs where success is found. The difference between me and you is dissection. Keep at the dissection business taught by Solomon till it lands you the naturalist's sanctum, the doctor's ward. Keep on till you are hard enough to cut open anybody and anything, regardless of their cries.

This is Solomon. If you like the Solomon way that is your lookout, but the way of Jesus Christ is not identified with the dissections of men and animals. It is only identified with the Heavenly fire, the entrancing elixirs of that other presence whose pulling beams of warmth and light draw up the fainting heart, upbear the drooping hope, uncover the shining divinity in the so-called wicked, show up the unteachable wisdom of the eternal soul of all.

Verses 11 and 12, "There was none like thee before thee, neither after thee shall any arise like unto thee."

It was well that none had ever before had such an idea of separating himself from other men as Solomon had. It is well that we shall not see his like again. It is good for the world that one came after him who could have had as many women under his thumb, as many armies under his eye, as great learning in his brain, but made nothing of the whole of them. He saw that unreality is not the starting place. Saw that to have no defined idea was greater than to stick to one great idea. It was well that Jesus bathed in the fires of universal inspiration.

Verses 13 and 14, "If thou wilt walk in my statutes I will lengthen thy days."

And Solomon held on to his idea or let it hold him, without interference, till, like a fever, it had had its run. But this run did not make him happy. His retainers used to hear him groaning so loudly with anguish of mind that they were afraid to go near him. It is never happifying to be a great discerner between good and evil people or events. It is never enchanting to have an idea running us as though we were wagons hitched to great horses, "Why do thoughts arise in your hearts?" asked Jesus when they got to discerning, separating, setting up and pulling down. And now notice, it is better not to give an idea its run, till we are like babies in its grasp. And the next time you get to suspecting or criticizing anybody, ask yourself the question, "Why do thoughts arise in your hearts?" and see what a quick treatment it will be to stop the pain of separating between good and bad. Back there where the father is there is no idea to run us. We touch the all-seeing light and to us all show their heavenly faces.

Verse 15, "And Solomon awoke and beheld it was a dream."

Do you suppose if it had been a reality he could have got him up hastily to kill some cows and lambs? How evidently it was the occult womb of skill in managing men and destiny he entered into, and not the radiant bosom of the tender God. We cannot say that in his times certain things were noble which in our times are heinous. This is the ruse of the prince. Believe him not. The changeless God speaks yesterday, today, and forever the same language.

This lesson turns us back to the Heavenly Fire from whose silent bosom we first hailed. Standing still in its flame we ask nothing. Standing still in its untold, moveless glory, we begin to breathe over again. The words of Jesus were about being born again, and they were true. Solomon was born again into the mysteries of occultism with its dominion over mankind and the machinery of money, apparel, marrying, slave owning, army furnishings, star gazings, and knowledge of plants. Jesus was born again into the mysteries back of the occult prince.

Stand still and be born, as He said, all ye people. Think not and so be started afresh to walk on the highways of the untold light.

The Heavenly fire is worth attending unto. But whoever is bathed in it is unambitious and unpretentious forevermore, though greater than Solomon.

Inter-Ocean Newspaper, October 11, 1896

LESSON III

The Mysterious Adeptship
Inherent In Us All

I Kings 4:25-34

It has been discovered that when the mind gets fused to one idea it rises to as free height as that idea is capable of going. At the moment when it is free it is melted, as it were, and whatever direction it then takes it runs to intense extremes. The first part of the programme is concentration, onepointedness. The second part is suggestibility, adeptship, waking trance, hypnotic determination.

Last Sunday we saw Solomon fusing his whole mind to the idea of being a great ruler over men, a strong intellect. This week we find the historian declaring that his "God gave him largeness of heart as the sands of the sea." All the learned commentators declare that this does not mean that he was generous and large- hearted, but only that he rose to a stupendous sense of his own importance. In his day the people had safety from foreign interference, but as he was an aristocrat by birth, breeding, and opportunity, his people said that though he had fine carriages and nearly a thousand wives to make all other rulers envious, still "he made their yoke grievous."

This lesson has for its main purpose to show how a ruler gets into a chair and how he fails or succeeds in knowing what to do with his chair after he gets into it. It refers to the incoming hour of Kingship, Presidentship, Czarship, etc., on this globe today, but it is also very sweet in its kindly voice to individuals at this hour showing them what method to pursue to keep out of the clutches of the aristocratic dynasty upon which we are now to enter as a temporarily taxed, and distinctly classed people on a swinging planet.

The golden text reads: "Them that honor me I will honor, and they that despise me shall be lightly esteemed." The verses to be applied to this age and section of time are to be found in I Kings, 4:25-34. The golden text calls attention to the mysterious adeptship inherent in us all. It says that if we will exalt any imaginary apothegm or aphorism by focalizing all our energies to it we shall get all the hot force we need to magnetize honors, riches, beauty, etc., to ourselves. But, of course, if we do not fuse, melt, focalize, all our energies of mind to any one principle we must be second rate, third rate, or even stupid sort of people.

This lesson is meant to intensify last week's lesson. It has a peculiar effect on anybody to read it over once. It intensifies the effect to read it over twice. The special treatment that radiates from it is to rouse us to make a clean-cut statement of what we are really trying to do in this stage of our experience. Are we making stones, politics, personal glory our goal of attainment? Do we want to be a leading mineralogist? Do we aspire to be President of the United States? Do we want people to love and believe in us? Something is really a subconscious chord in our mind and represents the thing we are straining after. This lesson strikes on that subconscious chord and by facing us up with it gives us a choice to take supreme interest of a very executive sort in the actual "something," whose business it is to make us no more victims to men or nature; whose business it is to make us expose unweighted, independent divinity.

Heretofore humankind has been hypnotized into believing in an overruling, all wise, all competent God who would not do one single act of kindness or interference with evil when they were in distress, unless they had superhuman faith in him.

The mind of mankind has been focalized, fused, to this idea concerning the Supreme Being. The idea has about run its race with mankind, and almost with one accord they are now insisting upon the active co-operation of that Omnipotent Energy which set them going on this planet, and some definite manifestations of his kindness, whether they have faith in him or not. This insistence will reach its acme in somebody, and that somebody will lead off a multitude of converts, who will be magnets to draw all the forces of nature and all the events of life to bring them favors. Life will no longer mean to them a series of strenuous endeavors to overcome conditions. It will be one joyous holiday of acceptance of the free gifts of a whole universe.

Such an announcement as this is treason to the former teachings about the Divine Father; but it is the actual teaching of Jesus Christ. Is it not in abundant evidence that our former teachings have been all upside down when we view the general state of the inhabitants of the world this moment? They cannot seem to rally any faith in the conquering power of men fighting for the right. Note how afraid each Christian nation is to tackle the little Sultan of Turkey and put a stop to the massacre of Armenians. Do you suppose any Christian nation would stand back if it had faith in the all-conquering power of a man or nation, armed firstly with guns, and secondly with right?

Why should frenzied Peter the Hermit have had such ability to rouse the minds of men to white heat over the idea of visiting the holy tomb? See what faith they had in the power of the right to win. But they had no eternal faith, for, like Solomon, it reached its zenith and waned, and no evidence that they were in the right, for the Mohammedans, who had charge of the holy things, believed themselves to be in the right, too. And though they all fought valiantly, the Mussulman won the day. The North believed it was in the right and the South believed itself to be in the right, too.

Each drew sword against the other to settle the question, and the North won the day. The subconscious chord of reason why no Christian nation now practically takes up the cause of the Armenians is because not one actually believes enough in the conquering power of the right to fight for it against great odds. For the day of fighting for right is closing. The era of expecting the right to take care of us and befriend us without our assistance is opening. The hour of standing still to see the salvation of the divine kindness is striking.

We make note that Solomon, having risen to a good height on an idea, was such a shining strength while its run was on that not a man had any power against him. Nobody could criticize him with any show of success. His enthusiasm over himself as a magnate communicated itself to his people. His reign of peace through fusing his mind to an idea was ante-type of the reign of peace which Jesus Christ ushers in through dropping ideas and letting the Original Power do its own way with us.

There is no enthusiasm, no white heat, where there is no idea of fighting, and no idea of lording it over our neighbors. There is only sweet tenderness, heartsome friendliness, which is so contagious that whether Christian or Turk sets the determined example, the other is bound to catch the spirit.

There is no evidence that Solomon's idea was the absolute thing, because he flattened out when it had had its run. The absolute power does not have a run like a human life or a fever. It is eternal and changeless. Therefore Solomon's success must be regarded as symbolic, hinting at the eternal and changeless. Last week's lesson said that his enthusiasm was a dream. That is self hypnotism. This self-hypnotism ran so high that it roused all Jewry. This lesson proclaims that self-hypnotism is good at drawing things that standing free from selfhypnotism is ownership of the world in which he walks. As age came on, Solomon lost his grip. There is no age to come upon the naked, un-hypnotized soul. Solomon was not happy with his kingship. "The soul bathes its world with the eternal smile of a buoyant nature, to be exposed to us all as fast as the leading pioneer can radiate his un-hypnotized quality through space to dissolve our present trance.

This lesson concerning the susceptibility of large crowds to the hot idea of one mind is sustained by a writer in the October Century. His name is Boris Sidis. This is what he says: "In my experiments in suggestion made in the psychological laboratory of Harvard College, I found that when the attention in perfectly normal people was concentrated on one point for some time, say twenty seconds, commands suddenly given at the end of that time were very often immediately carried out by the subjects. Concentration or attention on one point is highly favorable to suggestion."

The peculiarity of Solomon was that he superintended his own concentration and did his own suggestion. He had thought so intensely about himself that even in his dreaming: state his mind kept right on with the same subject. The height of attention is reached when the mind keeps up the same idea waking and sleeping.

This lesson exposes the fact that many times when people have thought they heard the voice of the absolute and changeless God, they have only heard the voice of their own strongest idea. The golden text shows it from the outset. It is only a naked idea that is so revengeful and so rewardful as to bless me when I let it have its way, to run me up and down wherever it pleases, as if I were a child tied by a string.

The absolute and changeless God blesses me whether I am good or bad. He causes his rain to fall on the just and on the unjust. He tells Jerusalem that her warfare is accomplished and she shall have great peace, even though she has slain her prophets and stoned them that came with glad tidings. He does not say that it is righteous to kill and commit adultery in one generation, and wicked to do so in another. This lesson exposes the fact that men are only chasing an idea started up somewhere by some intense mind when they are contented with such sophistries. This lesson is intended to wake us up and set us free from being hauled around by ideas of any sort.

Verse 25 says that the Jews dwelt safely under their own rooftrees all the days of Solomon. Yes; they were protected by the paw of Solomon's power. Nobody but he dared molest them. As he was not a cruel monarch like Nero, but only a self-aggrandized one, they said he did not hurt them by swords and gibbets but only taxed them heavily. He was under the orderly run of his main idea, and as he himself felt safe and secure, so he let his so-called inferiors, namely, the people not sitting on thrones, feel well protected, too. The absolute and changeless God does not give me my protection under the taxing paw of a pompous aristocrat, but shows that great personage very plainly that there is nobody above me and nobody below him. This lesson is meant to show us all the effect of following an intense idea of high and low, bad and good and the effect of letting go an idea and giving the impartial Presence its exposure.

Verse 26 says that Solomon had fifty-two thousand horses. This verse is intended to show how prompt and strong a great idea compels everything to be in serving itself. There is a law of attentiveness of mind to the word "friend" as it is written on a card, whereby all people who come to see the person whose mind has let go of everything but that idea of "friend" rouse all their best energies to befriend him. Solomon's idea was fifty-two thousand horse power, to be sure, but it was not a bit stronger than a poorhouse woman's idea would be, if she would concentrate as intensely as he did. Solomon stands up on the pages of holy writ to show the common energy of an idea. But let it not be supposed that Jesus stands upon its pages to show any such thing. He did not keep a psychological laboratory to teach the power of ideas. His mission was to show mankind how to shake free from the psychology of suggestions from all quarters.

Verse 27 says that the whole business of all the officers was to feed Solomon. Certainly. Everything will minister to the idea of self-consequence when it is not mixed with any idea of weakness or ignorance. The trouble with pretentious people, whom we do not serve with alacrity, is that they do not concentrate so hotly as to melt down those stubborn little ideas of weakness and ignorance that keep raising their little heads as long as they can. Solomon had melted those two little notions. Do not think that the food and drink and shelter furnished by the Jesus Christ quality is drawn from the possessions of the people by the magnetic attraction of a brilliant personality glittering by reason of a well- freed idea. No; the ministry to the free soul cometh from the angels to every man equally. Those officers dared not complain in the presence of magnificent Solomon, but in their secret hearts they knew that the people felt his paw to be grievous heavy. Of course it is called transcendentalism, when one brings up the mention of all men being equally well provided for and nobody feeling that he is the inferior or superior in position or knowledge anywhere he may go. But it is the actual effect of ceasing to be hauled and mauled by other people's focalized minds.

Verse 28, 29, and 30 say that Solomon threw off original sayings from his shining idea as a sun throws off asteroids. When a man says new and strange things we know he has an idea which is not mixed with other notions as thickly as other people's minds. Pretty soon we all begin to be trained around by his speeches, as all the religious mothers for three thousand years have been whipping their children thoroughly to keep up with Solomon's directions, and all the religious men for three thousand years have declared that sorrow is better than laughter, just because Solomon said so.

Verse 34 closes the section that applies to what is already settled in the minds of our people, which is to expose itself outwardly pretty soon. This verse says that Kings came to see Solomon's high idea fling its original things around. This is as high as an idea can get. At this point it began to wane in Solomon. There is not a single idea that a mind can concentrate itself upon that will not begin to wane when it gets the highest minds of other men to admiring it. It is the same as the sun of our sky, which begins to set when it touches the zenith. But there is a sun that never sets. It is the unspeakable will of the impartial Presence. It is the untold glory of the supernal Intelligence. It makes no difference if all our Governors, Presidents, Princes have ignored this impartial Presence, seeking ever to rule us to their own advantage, till all mankind are saying human nature runs that way, and we cannot stop it; the fact remains that there is one standing in our midst forever whose substance is the bread to eat and never wanes. No description touches this Presence. No idea fits any beauty or wisdom of this Presence. No king is nearer than you to this Presence. No saint lies on a pillow closer to the bosom of this Presence than any sinner's pillow. For it is the Impartial One. Hear, ye heavens, and give ear, O, earth; your God dwelleth among you.

Though Solomon, in all his glory struck dismay to Kings, a greater than Solomon is here. Who is there to catch this heavily groaning age with its distinctions of high and low, rich and poor, under the mesmerism of the reigning suggestions of combined kingship, the influence of the Impartial One now standing in, our midst? Who can shake himself free from the determined positions taken by the monarchs of this age to hold their own advantages regardless of the rights of others, and by shaking himself free from being like them in any respect lave himself in the influence of an unfading unwaning, all- competent, all-providing majesty?

The Bible teaches that such an impartial Presence is always here. It teaches that whoever is absolutely un-hypnotized, either by himself or anybody else, can breathe enough of this unwaning One to be the joyous light of the world.

Inter-Ocean Newspaper, October 18, 1896

Lesson IV

Missing

LESSON V

Building The Temple

I Kings, 5:1-12

The subject of this lesson is "Building the Temple." The topic for consideration is "Solomon's Zeal." The golden text is "Except the Lord build the house, they labor in vain that build it." The verses to impress the subject are to be found in I Kings, 5:1-12. The fact to remember in the Solomon campaign, election, and administration is that Solomon was an aristocrat, with a lofty idea of himself, which he palmed off on the Jews as the changeless and everlasting God of heaven.

In throwing aside all written and well-accepted interpretations of Bible texts, and permitting the undefiled will of intelligence within us to spring forth to understand Solomon's position we are like liberated subjects from the snares of hypnotism. For the original intelligence within us is bold to declare that it was in no sense whatsoever the changeless Absolute in his admirable character with whom Solomon conversed in his dream, and

43

rose up to kill some helpless animal to show his praise of him. It was in no sense whatsoever the mighty one dwelling in holy eternity with whom Solomon talked, and rose up, determined to make the yoke of several million Jews grievous to be borne and also enthused to expose to other Oriental monarchs like splendors of an unprecedented and uncopyable harem. No. The direct, invariable affect of face to face meeting with the God who is beyond all ideas of man is to make us willing to leave all living things in happy free life. It is to make us chaste, unobtrusive, and unpretentious. It is to make us see plainly the equality of divinity at the center of all men, and compel us to address it in such a fashion that no man regards us as holding any whip hand over him, and we can never, under any circumstances, feel that any human being or combine of human beings, has any whip hand over us.

Solomon was self-hypnotized. With his own hypnotic trance he hypnotized the whole body of Israelites with whom he dealt during a long and brilliant period. At the end of that time his hypnotizing idea began to decline, as all ideas do after certain run. It is not generally known that ideas have their appointed runs like fevers and mumps. Whoever gets into the clutches of an idea is hauled and mauled by it in such a way that he is as much a child in its grasp as Solomon said he was in the clinches of his idea as related in I Kings, 3:7. We all remember how Napoleon's idea began to decline in its intensity when he was 42 years of age, and landed him on St. Helena's last couch in the year 1821. His idea was very similar to Solomon's. It was his main notion to sit in supremacy over his fellow men, and this notion was so strong that it enlisted his whole faith that he was able to do it. This idea became his god, exactly as Solomon's idea was his god. Napoleon said he was a man of destiny. So did Solomon. Of course, they were, exactly as every fever or whooping cough having its free whip hand with us gives us perforce a destiny just like itself.

The Solomon lessons are set like blue diamonds into the mystic gold of sacred story to teach me that I am to be a little child in the bonds of something supremely grander than an idea; something that will shine brighter and brighter, until in some perfect day, I know the night no more forever, either in my intelligence or my surroundings. Solomon's idea waned like a gorgeous summer day. Napoleon's idea waned likewise. But that to which I am cemented hath no wane.

Solomon's idea dragged him down so that, as these lessons have before told his misery of mind was so profound that sometimes his retainers were afraid of him, he groaned so loudly. Napoleon's idea in its wane dragged him down so that at the Elba battles he rouged his cheeks to hide his pallor and marched back and forth from Silesia to Bohemia, wearing and tearing his strength in futile efforts to accomplish victories, which his falling idea could never more nerve him to.

These Solomon lessons say that at the hour when the great people of the world have heard of us and come praising us, then is our downfall at hand, if we are built up by an idea. At that juncture the flaws in our character begin to be represented. If our heart is cemented to the divine that supersedeth ideas, then every flaw shall be our glory instead of our shame. Every defeat shall help spread our sunshine instead of clouding it. Every enemy shall be our fame, instead of our sorrow. The sweetness of David's character was due to his letting go of his own idea by snatches and thus giving the light of the unspeakable soul a right to shine through. But again he covers, and again covers, that splendid light with his own idea. The marvelous miracles of Moses are wrought just as he is free from the grip of his idea. The gentle gifts of Elisha are made when he is not presuming to hold an idea. The transcendent wonders wrought by Jesus were the swift and easy accomplishments of one who had never been touched by an idea. But Solomon kept his head true to his prevailing idea as long as he could wink or walk. Even in his dreams he remembered that his business was to surpass and to manage his fellow men. In the lesson which detailed his principal ambition (See Oct. 11) he is reported as being so melted to his idea as to hear it talk. This is finding the occult starting point of temporal things.

Anybody can hear his chief idea talk, if he is hypnotized enough by it. At that point Solomon charged up a little stone with occult energy, and for a great many years afterward that little stone gave its wearer power over demons or bad luck. This stone has bean called a seal. (See Lane, Arabian Nights, introduction, note 81, and chapter I, note 15.)

Everybody who has a mastering, hypnotizing idea has more or less influence on the minds and lives of his fellow men. Napoleon said he did not regard the sacrifice of a million men if he could win a battle. And France hurried and bore children by the multitudes and gave her grown-up men with eagerness, under the trancing influence of his trance. In the Literary Digest of Oct. 14, page 832, we find defeats in chess playing laid at the doors of the overpowering mind of the antagonist. That note is copied from the Times, Philadelphia, and speaks of Morphy as defeated by Paulsen3 in 1857, under the hypnotism of Paulsen.

In our age we are particularly susceptible to the powerful idea of some man or some woman advancing new theories and sustaining them determinedly, because we are so dissatisfied with the way the old ideas have turned out. All the poverty of this generation is due to the concentration of the whole mass on the subject of money getting led off by the Jay Gould and Rothschild type of humanity. In David's day he showed his bright soul only on the occasions when he stopped his own ideas. And, strange as it may seem to apply the same principle to chess playing, Morphy could not rally his wisdom except by taking his eyes off the board while Paulsen was making his moves.

The Bible lesson causes us to repeat the assertion made some weeks ago in this series, that the name Jesus Christ has in it a quality that takes our mind from the influence of mankind on every subject and leaves us to our own independent intelligence.

On reading over the notes of the present commentators on these Bible sections we see how each author is deeply entranced by the ideas of all his predecessors in writing interpretations. But by letting the liberating quality of the name of Jesus Christ annul their influences in our own case, we are able to see that Solomon did not talk with the Almighty Eternal One at all, but only with his waxing idea. We are able to see that, as Solomon's history is dished up for this particular season of national life, we are about to have an overpowering aristocracy handle the reins of our government for a swift period of time. Listen to the way the Encyclopedia Britannica, page 416, speaks of Solomon's administration. It represents the main idea of the administration we now enter: "His aim was less the advantage of his subjects than the benefit of his exchequer. His passions were architecture, a gorgeous court, and the harem, in which he sought to rival other Oriental kings." For this he required copious means — tribute in kind and money. On the basis of the firmer administration now introduced, stability and order could rest. Judah had no cause to regret the acceptance of this yoke. Closer intercourse with foreign lands widened the intellectual horizon of the people. But it need not be denied that mischievous consequences of various kinds slipped in along with the good.

For by holding the yoke of a magnetizing idea over a taxed and hard- pushed people we see the ten tribes subconsciously preparing to revolt under Solomon's son, Rehoboam. This, as a former lesson proclaimed, is inevitable wherever a Solomon holds away. In our day Solomon and Rehoboam must be fused into one administration, for the ten tribes, are not subconsciously preparing to revolt. They are already rumbling their conscious determinations not to be yoked to any golden charioted alliances of potentates.

This Bible section declares that it is vain to have battalions and money to bolster up an idea after its decline has begun, but that that which is beyond ideas can accomplish the utmost miracles without battalions or money. Notice carefully the golden texts "Except the lord build the house, they labor in vain that build it." We know that "Lord" is a word that means ruling idea in all cases, but applies often to the Changeless and Eternal One as an influence. In this golden text; it applies to both. If the masterful idea is on the wane, no amount of soldiers or money will win the day. See how much better equipped Napoleon was with assistants after he began to fall than before. But if it is not an idea that is running us, but the living and unvarying God, there is no wane, and so we are kept by the Lord, of whom the word Lord only intimates when it is used in most books. If we speak of the Lord we must define whether we mean a governing idea or the supernal, unaltera- bly kind God of whom no idea can be formed.

The people tell sometimes of the hand of the Lord in the campaign of Americans scrambling to put a certain man into the Presidential chair. They would discover, if they investigated more closely, that it was the magnetizing, powerful idea of a goodly body of people focused into one man, perhaps first emanating from himself, that was running him into the chair, it was having its run like a strong fever. Cleveland surely went into his place on an idea. Wherever the unspeakable and indescribable Lord is watched we find as the out- come universal prosperity, no favoring of a set few against the masses; no founding of combines, trusts, monopolies, to by and by strike the crowds with their ruthless fangs. Perhaps we have never seen a president put up by anything except an idea having its feverish run. Most certainly the state- ment by a man that he is a man of destiny is not to be taken as an evidence that he is watching the changeless kindness of the every present One, whom ideas cannot reach. It generally means, as in Napoleon's case, that he feels the clutch, the grip, the pull, of his prevailing idea at its high swing. If it is all there is of him he can hear it talk as Solomon did. It would be a good plan to be de-magnetized from these men's ideas utterly for a while, so that, like Paul Morphy at the chess board, we might have something original in our judgment.

The first verse of the chosen section tells how Hiram, King of Tyre, sent messengers to Solomon, the golden charioted ruler of his countrymen, to congratulate him on having secured the throne. Wealth and power always shake hands with wealth and power. They are drawn together like richly attired ladies at afternoon teas; like learned people at receptions. Fraternities are formed on the principle of like attracting like. All these things are emblems, symbols, of the droughts of the pure unquenchable flame of the Soul on the everlasting Soul of the skies and the spaces.

> "Where soe'er in glory gliding
>   Shine the stars on nights of time,
> There the mystic magnet hiding
>   Draweth toward it soul of mine."

If the Soul be wedded to the Soul, consciously, so that we notice how cemented it is, we shall not be mere interested in the gorgeously dressed than in the ragged. We shall not be more pleased by the man who knows the infinitesimal calculus than the woman who knows how to wash flannels. We

shall be watching the soul spark in them, recognizing ourself, our God, our partner for eternity, in
that unquenchable fire of which they themselves
have never even heard.

Verses 2 and 3 tell how Solomon began to draw
upon his friend for aid at once, just as consciously
or unconsciously insects do begin to spring around
to catch on to the right storehouses, and if they are
strongly charged with drawing quality, like
France, hurrying and straining to help Napoleon
glorify himself, all things will jump and make
haste to add to their pleasure.

Every idea is drawing, or magnetic. Let a person get the idea that he is unlucky and he will
magnetize his affairs so that every turn he makes
will work against him. People will unwittingly
throw disadvantages in his way. This idea will
have its run, like a fever, get to its end and die
out. Can a man check an idea and stop its course
with him? He can. He can willfully change his
idea. Does the Bible teach changing ideas as the
supreme business of man? No. It teaches to stop
from having any ideas till whatever we say or
think works quickly and accomplishes itself so
plainly that we know just what we are about in
the mind realm as in the material realm. This
state of sitting on the throne and handling ideas
as we handle our fingers and ears has not been
well reached because we have let ideas handle us
just as Solomon did. No matter how good the idea,
remember it is not the true God. And no matter

how kingly powerful the help and re-enforcement we get while being run by an idea, it ia not the eternally reliable way of re-enforcing ourselves.

The rest of the verses detail the mutual benefit, which the kings become to each other by having a common object of interest. To the King of Tyre the God of David was probably an invisible idol, and as he believed greatly in idols he was glad to help erect a temple to the idol of his neighbor King. The intimation, therefore, is that Solomon's concept of God was no higher than Hiram's, for in due season the temple fell to pieces. The temple which the quenchless soul dictates the building of is not decidable. And it is possible to stand back at the soul throne of our being and build such an edifice. Hiram and Solomon were great Kings, but they knew not that the quenchless soul of fire dwelt in all their subjects, therefore they disappeared into the glooms of death. They knew nothing diviner than the occult starting places of things, so all their accomplishments were for their own glorification as strong minds. Therefore when their minds fainted, they fainted too. The further details of the story of two kings of a feather building a temple to an idea are only the filling in to call attention to their success and its temporal nature. Solomon's seal was the bold concentration of all his mind to his notion of lording it over his fellow men by superior knowledge of occult matters. Such zeal is no more commendable than Herrmann's enthusiasm over sleight-of-hand experiments, or Keeley's over his motor. They are not out of the range of any human mind concentrated on any one subject till the subject talks back.

It is all vanity till that which is nobler than the mind can conceive is in full sway. Solomon himself was intensely mental, and therefore magnetized unto himself all that the mind can know and all the power that the mind can have. But the mind is as much of a setting and rising planet as the body. The utmost zeal we can rally to melt our mind to power along any line is only a limited commodity. No matter how the saints trained themselves, they got decrepit in both mind and body after the lapse of years, and even the buildings they founded are crumbled at this date. Stranger than that, the noblest principles their minds could enunciate while at white heat of enthusiasm, feeling most positive that the absolute and true God had dictated them, are coming now to be seen as no use for our age or people.

If those principles had been the face-to-face announcements of the unalterable One, do yon suppose they would have been good for past generations but bad for our generation?

When David sawed his captives alive, as he felt certain his God had decreed, was he nearer right than Queen Victoria would be to-day doing the same thing? Let no man say he has a revelation from the Almighty, simply because his own idea talks back to him. Let only the man who can stand

up and accomplish the impossible without thinking how to do it and without trying to be anything
dare to foist upon our age any theorem or axiom or
aphorism. Not one of them has any power in itself.
It is only an idea, over which he is enthusing,
which will do its utmost in his case and leave him
stranded later on. Solomon cried out in anguish
that all his proverbs were vanity, all his regalia
was vanity. Would he have cried out that the living God was vanity if he had ever felt consciously
the glorious rush of his holy spirit?

There was one announcement of Jesus to
which we may attend: "If I do not the work of the
Father, believe me not." Did Solomon set the value
of his slaves equal to his own value? Yet, without
doubt, if he had felt the heavenly fire burning from
contact with the mighty God, he would have made
the slave equally powerful with himself. Did Solomon call the Jews to make Omnipotent Holiness
their king, and not himself? Yet that is what contact with holiness does. "Henceforth I call you not
servants, but friends," said Jesus. For, he had
breathed into his nostrils the breath of the real
God and was a living soul.

There are signals by which we may know when
a man has breathed into his nostrils the heavenly
fire of the Lord God Omnipotent. He is free from
the world and its trials, and his presence is freedom for his neighbors. The light of his eye is
health and prosperity for them. The sound of his
voice is the healing music of heaven. The touch of

his hand is the awakening of long-stilled hopes. The heart and the mind sing a new song when he appears. He is utterly unlike Solomon.

Inter-Ocean Newspaper, November 1, 1896

LESSON VI

The Dedication Of The Temple

I Kings, 8:54-63

With me faith means perpetual unbelief,
Kept quiet, like a snake 'neath Michael's foot,
Who stands calm just because he feels it writhe.
- Browning

The subject for contemplation during the coming week is "The Dedication of the Temple." It explains the service which preceded the completion of the temple built by Solomon. The policy of the reign of Solomon is hereby announced, and very nearly all the Jewish people signify their assent by falling on their faces in deep belief that prosperous days are ahead of their nation because Solomon, who believer in governing men with grievous yokes, has now got hold of the reins of state with firm determinations. (See I Kings, 8:54-63)

As these lessons are all positively applicable to our day and generation, we can tell just how notable our Nation is now about to seem in the estimation of other nations, and by noting exactly how the masses regarded Solomon's handling of them we are able to see just how the mass of people are to feel about the definite government to which they now come in our age. That there is to be strength and splendor at headquarters is sure. The other nations will do the government that carries the ark of this age immense honor is certain. That the ark of this age is not a chest overlaid with gold but a noble principle, is plain to everybody. That the only nation with an absolutely noble principle is our own has been told to us ever since we could comprehend our father's speech. That the noble principle reads, "All men are created free and equal," we all know.

This section of Bible story applies to us all individually in a strong or a weak fashion according as we are in the habit of attracting blessings in a strong or weak fashion. If we apply the lesson to ourselves, and let the Nation's affairs alone, we shall be independent of what is going on among the people at large. What happens to the world and to the masses will not interest us; but the lessons since July 1, have been laid out for national experiences, as well as personal events. So we will write their meanings large until the year is up. We will apply them to ourselves just the same. We can all be at the strong, splendid headquarters called Solomon's throne and temple. We can all ignore the report of insurrection among our people and their affairs in the lofty style of King Solomon and spread out our hands in prayer to our own idea of God, with just as good success as Solomon did, or we can strike for an unfailing God, superior to our concepts, as Solomon did not.

Browning's verse, which hits the keynote of Solomon's gorgeous calmness as it related to the multitudes whom he was ruling so vigorously, hits the real state of all the rulers' minds who are sitting on external thrones in our time; and it also hits the state of mind existing wherever any religious teacher is depending upon his knowledge of religion to bring him in his bread and butter. There is nobody set aside from this Browning verse, except such as are not in the arena with the rest of the world, scrambling to get high honors of praises from their neighbors and striving to be great minds by some superior knowledge of the High Hand that swings this universe.

Read Browning's verse over again. Watch great Solomon on his knees, praying to his concept of God. Watch him in after life, at his secret groanings. Note how the religion's teachers feel at the secret spring, where they know how little they know and feel how wary they have to be to get along and outdo their colleagues. Note how the kings, presidents, emperors are feeling about how the writhing oppositions to them are putting them to their mettle every instant. Read the verse over again:

"With me, faith means perpetual unbelief,
   Kept quite like a snake 'neath Michael's foot,
Who stands calm just because he feels it
writhe."

All these things show the same widespread un-
rest. They all show that there must be some spring
to touch which can enable us to sit still in our
houses and cease from holding our feet on snakes'
heads. That is holding down our fears and doubts
of mind and holding down our dissatisfied acquaintances and unsatisfactory affairs. The very
story of holding outward calm either of mind or
conduct while something plagues or scares them,
shows that there is a state where neither our mind
nor our affairs can touch us. If we fail to lick up a
little taste of the salt of unspeakable independence
we miss the actual streak in this lesson.

Remember, the subject is "The Temple Dedication." Take notice, the dedication service took
place before the temple was finished. Mark well;
the temple is our own independence of men,
events, minds, thoughts, feelings. Understand
plainly, the dedication is the recognition that this
entire independence of the world, the flesh and the
devil is our own by native birthright. Never forget
for an instant that there is not the slightest need
of marching around in the arena of human life to
hold our own with the world. And regard it as
kindly certain that from the instant we discover
that we really have a supreme right to independence all the common events of daily existence

begin to work to prove it and thus recognition of our rights is the dedication of our temple. Recognition of our right to independence goes ahead of the completed independence sometimes a long period, and so the dedication of Solomon's temple was some time before the temple was finished.

This recognition of the brilliancy and strength of his own idea of self-importance was Solomon's God. It was his understanding as far as it had risen. He talked to it as a child might talk to a king. He talked to it with the confident certainty that it was very competent. And we all know that Solomon's idea was very well worked up.

> "But there are signs by which we know
> Faithful friend from flattering foe."

The conversation of Jesus with the actual God brought forth very different results, vary different results in personal life from those Solomon got. Divine tenderness, holy purity, common brotherhood, were what Jesus caught from talking with the everlasting comrade whose presence is unfailingly close. Solomon somehow managed to lose these effects. "By their fruits ye shall know them," whether they be simple concepts, or of God himself.

To hold the whip hand over men by reason of large money possessions or great book knowledge, or intense beauty, is nothing — nothing at all. As a flower of the field it passeth away. Solomon's whip hand was of this type. The thing this lesson calls upon us to note is, that "A greater than Solomon is here." The lesson is useless to us if we get not this flavor.

The verses we are to consider particularly opens with No. 54: "And it was so that, when Solomon had made an end of praying all this prayer and supplication unto the Lord, he arose from before the altar of the Lord from kneeling on his knees, with his hand spread up to heaven." This verse shows us how strong and reassured we always feel when anything or anybody that we have focused all our hopes upon responds favourably to us. We stand up as if we were their equals. Conversation equalizes. Solomon felt his concept of his own importance talking back to him in a friendly fashion. So he arose from kneeling on his knees before it.

Our concepts like to be praised. They are like plants in flower pots. They want the sunshine of flattery, the rain of thanksgivings. But the actual God, whose being is above our conceptions, is just as responsible to our complainings and whinings as to our praises. We may be too groveling in grief to rouse a sentence of praise, and only just manage to stretch up our hands into the empty spaces with recognition that the presence fills them, and this is sufficient. We may whine and lament like Job, and like as this marvelous One heard and helped Job, so he will lay into our way, the divinest blessings. Conversations with the Absolute One are not necessarily flattering to his majesty and grandeur. But the fruits of talking to the undescribable one are always the same. The character becomes tender, generous, gracious, recognizing the equal greatness and native intelligence of all men alike. The surroundings become harmonious and satisfactory. The happiness of all who associate with us comes smiling upon them. They fuel no grievous yokes. We feel none. Did Solomon get these results to himself or for the Jews of his time? Then his standing up in a friendly fashion with the invisible one he had been talking to was not indicative of comradeship with anything higher than his own intense passion to be a brilliant King.

The fifty-fifth verse says that he was so charged with the electric radiance of his own passionate love of brilliant domineering that he shed sparks and streams from it over the congregation of Israel. He shouted with a loud voice at them, and rained down upon them charges from his own quality till they were utterly convinced that he had his grand superiority over themselves as a gift from the inconceivable God himself. In our day this power is called hypnotic. The only way we may know hypnotic power from divine presence is when we have no feeling that the divine presence has given to anybody any advantage over us or any wisdom we ourselves have not caught straight from the original Source.

Those Israelites from that public day of exhibition of Solomon's extraordinary adoration of his own idea of kingship were his servile slaves. His words were the blessing, praising influence binding then to his chariot wheels as long as he lived.

But as soon as he stopped they saw their bondage. Eloquence is very apt to bind people to a man's ideas. And when a man calls his principal idea the Lord's, he gets a singular rope around the necks of his audience. On this account Jesus advised going into the closet to pray and there being eloquent before the Secret One who would do all things for all of us alike, not for some of our acquaintance more than for other.

Solomon declared in the fifty-sixth verse that it was the same Lord that Moses talked with whom he was addressing while he spoke before the people. This had the effect of lifting their attention off Solomon for a few seconds to a praiseful attitude toward a healing, helping, presence. Then Solomon reminded them of how stern and unyielding in the law the God of Moses was, and immediately they believed again in a power whose kindness was marvelous one instant, and his severity was terrible the next.

In the fifty-ninth verse he hinted at their having some rights as a people in common with himself, in the common cause of making other nations stand aside to give them peace from war and preserving each man in his place to serve Solomon with all he needed.

In the sixtieth verse there is a lifting up of the people's attention to the Eternal One, and it has the effect of making the people look higher than Solomon's mind's lofty concept. This very sentence helped them to recognize during his reign over them that the yoke he was laying upon them was a grievous one, but the effect of it was not prolonged enough to make them touch the great fact of there being One in their midst who could keep them free from Solomon's yoke, and give him no whip hand over them.

The other two verses tell with what jubilation they all ran forth from Solomon's splendidly successful effort at public hypnotism and at his dictation slew 22,000 oxen and 120,000 sheep, and with this noble business ended up the dedication of the temple.

The deep strain of music that peals through this story is full of information about how the thoughts of the strong men and women of all ages may fall powerless when they come near us. For who can fail to see how they were all preaching their own ideas and not the actual God when they told of God and how eager they have always been, and yea, verily, are now, to compel the rest of the world to think as they do and do whatever they want them to. Where has the preacher been who has shown each man how independent of his fellow men he is by divine right, how capable everywhere of being a law unto himself by reason of his oneness with the Absolute One? Who has said unto mankind that, at their center they are all as wise as the all-knowing God himself, it were better to converse with the mighty wisdom always speaking there than to be following around after other men and women trying to obey their directions?

Who has spoken of a presence so all-capable that at one signal from any one of the lowliest of men and women his bountiful hand would open, his tender guidance would lead out of hardship, his mighty strength would defend from king's yokes?

Who now believes that though a great multitude are bowing down to an idea with a heavy yoke in its fingers they can be free from service to that idea, free from the yoke in its fingers, and as grand as Divinity itself in their independence of the aristocratic government that now, by its masterly concentration of kingly purpose, stretches out its heavy hand, gloved with promises of prosperity and justice, over a Nation of men and women?

The anthem sounding through this Bible section pleads for individual understanding of a life and bounty out of the reach of governor's precepts and king's taxations. Its notes strike still sweeter chords. They tell of a life and prosperity due all men alike, which come not from labor with the hands, not from thoughts of the mind, not from preaching about anything, not from teaching anything, not from believing anything, but simply from face to face converse with the everlasting One, who owns all things and does not have to work in a shoe- shop or school-room or newspaper office, or anywhere else, for what he owns.

This lesson shows upon the wings of silent song that Solomon became exactly as powerful as his idea and fell to pieces with his idea through conversation with his idea, so we can show forth the power, intelligence, beauty, and immortality of the God whom no man hath described by face to face conversation with him.

The silent text of this lesson is; Conversation equalizes. When the mighty silence responds to our addresses we and the silent One are one.

Like Jesus, we think it not robbery to be equal with the silent One, for out of his splendid silence his answering voice stands us up on our feet vested with his own glory. This is the living anthem pealing through Solomon's story.

Inter-Ocean Newspaper, November 8, 1896

LESSON VII

Converse With The Actual God

Kings, 9:1-9

"All who call on God in true faith, earnestly from the heart, will certainly be heard, and will receive what they have asked and desired, although not in the hour or in the measure or the very thing which they ask yet they obtain something greater and more glorious than they had dared to ask."

Martin Luther

The above paragraph is truth. There are different ways of asking the Omnipotent One for assistance, but when the different ways count for nothing there comes an answer to every request in some fashion or other. The lesson today calls upon us to consider blessings, prosperities, storehouses, advantages. These all come upon people because they wish for them, and drew them toward themselves; as magnets draw steel filings.

Solomon is used again as an illustration of a superior human magnet. His idea of God is talking back to him again. It is plain enough that it is his personal and special idea of God that is talking back to him because the actual God never dickers and bargains with men or angels. The actual God blesses me whether I am good or bad, whether I am male or female, black or white. His rain falls on the just and on the unjust. His peace falls on angels and demons alike. The angels and the demons both fall into the bottomless pit of the Mighty One's nature and are heard of no more whenever they look his way.

There is no idea with such impartial ability in its fingers. Every idea is obliged to be re-enforced and bolstered up at intervals by renewed promises of obedience to it exactly as in this chapter Solomon's idea is crying out for re- bolstering. (Kings, 9:3-9) The actual God has an everlasting text to which I will call your attention. It is this: "The Lord is able to make the stand." The actual God gives me a Divine pillow on which to rest my mind. He gives it to all this world equally with myself. It is this: "It is God's business to attend to my conduct."

Job found this out. He said: "Thou knowest that I am not wicked. Thy hands fashioned me." Then again: "My witness is in heaven, and my record is on high."

If in any way Solomon sifted some of his old ideas about the necessity for a man's discriminating rigorously between right and wrong in with his idea of managing men like a god he might well expect to get conscience stricken. Conscience is a sort of quicksand that gets into a man's mind. Shakespeare found out that "Conscience makes cowards." Napoleon said that if conscience should get rein with him his own reign would cease.

The effect of converse with the actual God is to take away conscience. One feels, after watching the Eternal God, that his conduct is the influence of that unquestionable grandeur, and is no longer timid, apprehensive, or self- depreciating, for nothing ever cries with hunger or pain or distrust because of his conduct. Neither animals, children, men, women, angels. Something about him blesses, heals, quickens animals, children, men, women, angels.

If ever one of Solomon's wives or slaves, animals or colleagues, wept or died for him to please him, his God was not the actual God. This is not Church teaching, but it is truth. We ought to have one in our midst for a week or so whose converse was with the actual God, and not with his own idea of God. He would show men how to live entirely free from fear. There is no law of consequence, of words, or actions, if we converse with the actual God. It is all one thing that happens, and only one thing can happen and that is joy. "With thee is fullness of joy."

The very prayers of men in church prayer meetings are saturated with the Solomon fear of consequences of evil from turning away from God, but the fact is that if a man has ever once turned toward the true God, he cannot possibly turn away from him. Can it be possible that anybody would think for an instant that any man on earth could resist the Almighty? "I drew them with bands" and "there is none that can deliver out of my hand," saith the truth of the actual God.

Of course, this actual God has never been well preached and so mankind has not yet the slightest experience of what kind of a world we would be if somebody had arisen with determination to proclaim such a God. We have terrorized for thousands of years under the preacher's ideas of God, but one waft from the fact about God would be sufficient to make a world breathe free from terror. These lessons have already proclaimed that Solomon's actions after praying showed that he had never prayed to anything higher than his own idea, and now this lesson crowns the announcement. His idea cannot hold on to him, it asks him to hold on to it.

The shining secret of this lesson is the irresistible proclamation it makes that there is One who is able to hold on to us and keep us without any of our assistance There is a divine presence which makes all we do and say divine. There is a divine One here in our midst who cannot punish us for going wrong, for his way is all the way there is, and there is no right or wrong way about it. All is joy for everybody and everything where we are, and that is all there is about it. We ourselves are all joy, and that is all there is about it. Beasts, angels, and men, it is all one, they weep no more. They never fear again. Read up the promises to them that for once set heart on the actual God who has so much power in him that they can never get away from him if once they turn toward him. You will be astonished to find how far removed from tortures and deprivations such people are. The Bible holds these promises. Read them. Copy them. Leave out the talks about punishings and chastisings and tryings and testings and there you have the actual effects of addressing the Powerful One.

The golden text selected by the committee is a case of sudden wisdom about what would have happened to Solomon if he had prayed to something higher than his idea. This is it. "The blessing of the Lord it maketh rich and he addeth no sorrow with it."

Solomon had finished building a temple to his idea of God and was as rich and learned as he could get to be under such a Lord. Then he began to lose interest in it and there was nothing in it strong enough to arouse him. He said: "Whatsoever mine eyes desired I kept not from them," yet it was all vanity.

These lessons have latterly put object lessons before us of a sort to make us seek for something truer, more reliable, more comfortable than what the men and women were experiencing, as described by them. Who has ever ceased to wonder how Solomon could have let go of his God if he ever took joy in his God, and truly there is no explanation of it until we find that he hid the actual God by his idea of God. It then became very plain that he is an illustration of mind at its best human stretch and not an illustration of the character of the actual God operating with man.

The lesson then hints at the peace and strength that come with all answers to prayer addressed to the actual God. "The blessing of the Lord it maketh rich, and he addeth no sorrow with it." This, certainly, as Martin Luther puts it, is more glorious than the saints of this world have ever dared to ask. For it is the custom on this earth to feel that there is a snakelike danger lurking in the folds of all prosperity. The saints have taught us to believe this. All the lesson commentaries on Solomon teach it. But the Solomon story itself does not teach it. The Solomon story teaches that when the Mighty One begins to rain prosperity on our heads it is of a sort that cannot pull us into questionable conduct, speech, or thought. It is an undefiled and glorious as the hand that sends it. It is as grand in reflex offset upon ourselves as the direct influence of its giver.

In all metaphysical instruction there is a phase of information by contraries. They tell us that we do not need to sleep and this puts us to sleep. They tell us that we do not need to be cured of anything and this lifts us out of pain and disease. They give it to our mind as silent contrary suggestion. This Solomon series has run the same line and has the same effect of turning us toward the God who is able to make us stand when we read of Solomon's Lord who threatened with such direct calamities if he did not stand.

Michael sang it about the true God when he cried: "Who is a God like unto thee passeth all transgressions?" According to this international selection we see that there is now a short period of rich answers to our past prayers, whether to our idea of God or to God himself. If answers are from the actual hand there is no shaky temptation enfolded. If from our ideas of the hand there is a conscious stirring that we fear we are not as devoted to spiritual things as formerly, we fear some punishment. The commands therefore, that we announce that all our blessings are given from the unspeakable fountain and not from our firm notions of any sort, and that they contain no temptations toward silly conduct, silly thoughts, or silly speech. It is the hour for announcing that our God is able to make us stand and does make us stand so that we fall not.

Verse 1 reads: "And it came to pass, when Solomon had finished the building of the house of the Lord and the King's house and all Solomon's desire which he was pleased to do.

It took Solomon twenty years to build the Temple and his own palace. Four of the years of his reign he spent in planning and sending out messages to other kings and friendly workmen and merchants, seven and a half years for the building of the Temple, and then thirteen years more to finish the palace, so he had been King of Israel twenty-four years when this lesson opens. At this point he has satiety of blessings, advantages, prosperities and now at this crowning place he gets afraid that something is wrong about himself. All that he had ever desired arrived. All his prayers are answered, yet something is scaring him.

After having read over the Bible lessons of the past few weeks, we are intelligent as to why Solomon sorrow sifted in with the prosperity. The blessing of the actual God maketh rich and addeth no sorrow with the riches; then Solomon did not get his riches directly from the actual God, but only from his own hot notion of what he wanted God to be, whoa he got his gorgeous palace, his matchless Temple, his worldly fame, his splendid harem, so fulfilling all his "desire which he was pleased to do."

In making careful note of the modern interpretation of ancient metaphysics, we now see that for the most part the propositions scarcely run one hair's breadth away from Solomon's stamp of wind. The adherents are all bent upon declaring what is to be done, to show up, to "demonstrate" the way they think up within their minds. But Jesus and Solomon thought differently. Jesus said: "Not my will, but as it is in heaven, so let it be on earth." Can anybody suppose that in heaven there are such conditions as Solomon thrust upon Jewry by his splendid mentality 1000 B.C.?

Verse 2 declares: "That the Lord appeared to Solomon the second time, as he had appeared unto him at Gibeon."

As "Gibeon" means "hill", we are to take the text as signifying that Solomon was in an exalted state of mind again, as he had been twenty-four years before, and the chief burden of his idea was again as it had been then, about surpassing his fellow-men and holding the reins of government over them. But this time he brings another idea to keep his first one company. It is the same self dis-trust which even now keeps other men from being as powerful and doing as grandly as they wish they might. And there is no ability in an idea to thaw down that self-distrust unless the whole will is engaged. So here we have Solomon, even in a Gibeon state of mind, hearing his two ideas talk-ing back to him. Listen.

Verse 3: "And the Lord said:

Verse 4: And if thou wilt walk before me to do all that I have commanded.

Verse 5: Then will I establish the throne of thy kingdom upon Israel forever.

Verse 6: But if ye shall at all turn.

Verse 7: Then will I cut off Israel out of the land, and Israel shall be a by-word."

Here at his Gibeon Hill of mind Solomon is not fused enough to his first idea so that he cannot hear anything else. He feels the notion of power which has sustained him in gathering palace, temple, fame, and harem, but it has lost its hold on his will. Any notion that men can praise up will act the same as Solomon's notion. After a time it faints, palls, stales. During the whole twenty-four years he had given his hearty co-operation to the notion of surpassing all other men with intellect, wives, temples, and palaces. Now his prayer, his desire is answered, but the palling motion is now companioned by fear. Solomon had not known that this self-distrust, this fear was in his mind before. He is astonished. He hears its threats. He hears his notion of power promise everything splendid if he will drop his self-distrust, but there are not many people who can quench fear when they have lost interest in their idea of achievement. If anybody feels that he has got about everything the world can give, how can he melt and smelt and wield all his will of mind to getting anything? His natural state of mind at this point is fear, dread, apprehension.

History shows how Solomon's fear triumphed. All its threats were fulfilled. This lesson declares that now is the moment to recognize that there is divine inner flame that cannot die. Its name no man knoweth, but whoso letteth it guide his life liveth in noble security from threats of failure. At the moment when this inner flame talketh to a man so that he knoweth its voice, he never heareth anything about managing his fellow men or surpassing them in any fashion. He never heareth it promise him to wipe out nations for his sake if he serves it, or to bring nations under his yoke, or to wipe him out with his nation of obedient followers, if he lets go from serving it. He can only hear from it while the suns endure and the stars revolve, one story only. Do you know that story? It is this:

"The Lord is able to make the stand."

"Before the day was I am be, and there is none that can deliver out of my hand."

"I will work and none shall hinder."

"I know the thoughts that I think toward you, thoughts of peace and not of evil."

"One God did make all men, of one-blood all the nations."

"There is no high or low, rich or poor, bond or free, male or female, black or white,

in me."

"I am the imperial One."

"1 am he that maketh rich and addeth no sorrow with it."

"Look unto me and be ye saved, all ye ends of the earth."

"In me shall all the nations of the earth be blessed."

Inter-Ocean newspaper, November 15, 1896

LESSON VIII

Reward Of Obedience

Proverbs 3:1-17

"Were I so tall to reach the pole
And grasp the ocean with a span,
I would be measured by my soul.
The minds standard of the Man.-
Dr. Watts

The golden text of today's lesson is: "In all thy ways acknowledge him, and he shall direct thy paths." It is the sixth Verse of the chapter which millions of Sunday-School scholars, will be considering today, viz. Prov. 3:1-17.

The title of the lesson is, according to the Sunday-school masters: "Rewards of Obedience." The title of the lesson is, according to its more esoteric meaning: "The Third Presence in the Universe."

This Third Presence is designated in this third Proverbs by the pronouns, "He, She, It." In many parts of the Bible this wonderful One is called "Him". In many parts "Her". In parts "It".

The Egyptians spoke of the Third Presence as "He". Champollion1 found on a ruined Egyptian temple this text: "He is by himself, yet it is to him that everything owes existence."

There is a different atmosphere and countenance about a human being whose attention is much fixed on the Third Presence in the universe. He counts for more than the ordinary. He swims out of difficulties better. He is more spontaneous. He needs less instruction from his neighbors. He is a walking proof of this golden text: "In all thy ways acknowledge (It or Her or) Him, and (It or She or) He will direct thy paths." A path is a line which we get to walking in. Wherever we are walking, whether in affluence or poverty, security or danger, it is the path we once elected to walk in. Our election of the path we are in was made consciously or unconsciously. This day's chapter tells us that if our heart" is set on the mighty He we shall find ourselves in a path that will give us joy every instant. "He" is quite able to push us, lead us, drive us into our most desirable path. The Bible is full of accounts of how handsomely we come on if we cast ourselves on the directing Hand of "Him".

Beethoven looked to the One who is by himself for direction on his path of instrumental music. Jenny Lind looked to the One who is by himself for direction on her path in vocal music. Lincoln looked to the One who is by himself for his direction on the path of equalizing men before the law

in a slave- holding government. Quimby looked to
the One who is by himself for his direction on the
path of curing men's minds of fixed notions about
their bodies.

This golden text says: "In all thy ways acknowledge him," as though Beethoven, Lind,
Lincoln, and Quimby looked toward him for one
kind of result on one of their ways, but did not
according to their own notions on other matters.
Beethoven could have got good ears if he had
looked to the "Him" for them. Lind might have
kept her judgment if she had looked to the "Him"
for it. Lincoln and Quimby might have lived longer
among us if they had looked for life.

We see by the sixteenth verse that "She" gives
length of days and riches to whoever acknowledges
Her as doing such things. It is absolutely certain
that a man could sit still in his room and acknowledge the unlimited ability of the One who is by
himself to attend to all his affairs and all his affairs would run pleasantly and profitably. As in
verse 10; "So shall thy barns be filled with plenty."
As in verse 17; "Her ways are ways of pleasantness, and all her paths are peace."

Verse 7 says: "Be not wise in thine own eyes."
It is only this Third Presence who is wise. You are
not wise as you scramble about, pulling yourself
from infancy to old age. I am not wise scrambling
along the same path. But "He" is wise. Some say
that this Third Presence is situated in our heads.
Some say this Third Presence in situated in our

hearts. Some say this name is "I Am." Some say his name is "God." There is one fact most true, and that is that nothing is real, actual, endless, but "Him." All else is nothing. Nothing at all.

The joy of Dr. Watts2 was great when he found that a man as tall as from Great Britain to the North Pole would be, in consequence, nothing — nothing at all. His third quality would be, "He." Watts called the third quality "soul", "mind". He certainly was not talking about the mind which a man exhibits when he is stretching himself up to compete with his neighbors and beat them by cheating them or shooting them. He must have meant the divine quality that sometimes exhibits itself in a man's eyes when he does the magnani-mous, the fearless, the generous thing. The writer of this (Proverbs 3:1-17) was watching the shining light that glows in the eyes of one who yields his own external interests to his neighbors, with his own attention fixed on the One who will look out for all his interests and more than make up for what he gives away. To be generous or free-handed, without, at the same instant while we are giving away our possession, having our attention fixed on the One this lesson is talking about, is to be very nice, very good, in our own eyes, and to very shortly discover ourselves in poverty, disad-vantage, disgrace.

This works as a fact on even small items. Give away your cornfield with your eyes on the bounti-ful One and you will never miss the cornfield. Give away the cornfield because it is generous to give things away, and you will miss the money and the bread that cornfield is worth. The name of being generous is a miserable reputation. The name of drawing from on high is excellent, for it calls attention to the storehouse on high where all may draw alike.

"He is by himself, yet it is to him that everything owes existence."

Get the reputation away from yourself to "Him" and though you seem to be lost sight of you are really glorified. For in "His" greatness is my greatness wherever he is or whatever his name is. In "His" wisdom I am wise, whatever his name or wherever he dwells. Some say this "He," who is such a storehouse for men, is smaller than the point of the finest cambric needle. The Orientals say this. Some say that he is larger than countless millions of suns and rolling stars. The Occidentals say this.

The seventh verse goes on: "Fear the Lord and depart from evil." These interpretations have already shown that to fear the Lord is to keep the eye on Him alone. He is the only storehouse. "He" is the only wisdom, the only strength, the only grandeur. Nothing else counts. Fearing is fixing the attention upon one thing and excluding all other things. This seventh verse says that we immediately depart out of the tracks of evil by fixing the expectations above. No cyclones of sorrow visit one who expects the mighty Him to do great and wonderful kindness to him. No cold winds of adversity ever blow on the heads of them that expect the all-owning Him to take care of them.

Some say that the wonderful "It" is the good. Some say no, "It" sends the good. Some day the wonderful "She" is truth. Others say no, "She" is the giver of truth. Why is all this disputation? Can you not see that it is because people are stopping to praise themselves by seeming to be in the right in the estimation of their neighbors and so not finding their supreme business of fearing the Lord or fixing their attention on high? Whosoever feareth the Third Presence in this universe careth nothing about being in the right or in the wrong. His eye is single to something which is above right and wrong.

Right and wrong are relative. "He is by himself." Those who have their eyes on the right and wrong are relative; they are not single-eyed; they are looking two ways; they are double-minded; they are double-eyed. Whoever is single-eyed to the mighty Third cannot go wrong. Whatever he does is divine. How can he worry about being blamed for wrongdoing or gasp for praise of rightdoing? This looking to him that sitteth alone by himself above right and wrong is fearing the Lord.

The word "Lord" has many applications in the scriptures. It is often used as governor, often used as the unidentified One, as in this verse.

The eighth verse declares that the single-eyed have deep-seated health. The starting point of their flesh becomes sound. The starting point of their bones becomes sound. This chapter does entirely away with the doctrine of right and wrong, health and disease, up and down, rich and poor, as subjects for study. If I am eager to help the poor, I am double-eyed. I do not fear the Third One, who is the Only Reality, for I am discriminating between two powers, viz., rich and poor. My flesh cannot be healthy, my bones ditto. No one ever saw a good, healthy philanthropist.

This lesson makes it very imperative as the starting point of unassailable health that we be not interested in the poor, not interested in the rich, not interested in the young, not interested in the old, for this He is not healthy either to bone or sinew; but if we are interested in him that is neither poor nor rich, sick nor well, young nor old, we shall be very superb radiators of equal health and beauty to every set of people everywhere we go.

If one should actually understand this chapter as it means, he could not keep on giving his money to hospitals and poorhouses, for he would see that he was actually making sickness and poverty by petting them and pampering them. He would find that the mighty Third One, the Lord of this chapter, would make him so healthy and so capable that the so-called sick in the hospitals would scramble instantly out of them; the so-called poor in the almshouses would flee to the homes that belong to them. Something would suddenly happen everywhere. This is true. The ninth and tenth verses sustain it. Honor him with thy substance, so shalt thou utterly overflow. If the eyes are on the Lord as the substance is given, there can be poverty no more. "When saw we thee an hungered?" asked the almoners. Of course, they never had seen the Lord Christ while handing out their buckets of soup. They had seen poverty-stricken wretches with one eye and richly fed nabobs with the other eye.

Jesus Christ saw the mansions prepared for all. He kept his eye on them. Whosoever looked at him and whosoever He looked upon ceased to be poor, ceased to be sick. This is truth.

Verse 11 declares that the son must never despise the chastening and the reproving of the Lord. Old commentary on this verse makes it seem that the Mighty One leans over from his happy throne and thrashes human beings often and severely in order to make them love him. Higher commentary proclaims that chastenings and reprovings that fall like incense from the Mighty One are the whitenings and renewals, evidences of the all-competent Friend of Humanity. One gets white, with the Holy Ghost, who watches the Third Presence. "My son" is my idea. Every one of my ideas is "my son". I will not have my ideas running around among poorhouses one moment and palaces the next. I will fix my eyes on the everlasting One, who sitteth above poor houses and palaces. So shall my ideas be chastened from relatives; chastened from high and low, rich and poor, black and white. So shall my ideas be whitened into a white breath from on high.

"Re" is a prefix meaning "over again." "Prove" is a word meaning evidence. The high One above evil and good proves over again, over again, and yet again, his ability to set every creature into unmolested happiness. Nobody can criticize this division of the word, "reproof," for it is what the mighty One convinces every one of us he doth do whenever we turn to face him and thus find out what he does mean. This eleventh verse declares that we cannot be weary, cannot dispose the loss of our ideas into the white breath of the Third Presence in this universe. It is as if I should say, using the old form of expression; "My ideas be never weary of joy in transmutation."

Verse 12 declares that love and delight are the effect of strict singleness of heart. If there should be any one way in which life could be more delightful to us than by any other line, let this verse be the assurance to the wonderful Third. This would certainly be called a "reward" by the scripture commentators, and "reward" is as good as any other name to call it by. The sun shines on the violet and it shows up its fragrance.

It is a reward to the violet for looking at the sun? This is exactly what happens if we look away from him that inhabiteth eternity, whose ways are not as our ways, whose thoughts are not as our thoughts.

Verses 13 and 14 tell of his happiness, this keen intelligence, this increase of prospering benefits that fall like sunshine, manna, balm, glory, upon one who is not interested in distinguishing between right and wrong, whose eyes are fixed on high.

Who was the divine radiance, the Quaker who condemned his neighbor for wearing a green hat band or the condemned Quaker who had been so happy in following his inner voice that he had not known of his hat being banded with green? One was double-eyed. One was single-eyed. The single-eyed one feared the Lord, and shone like a sunbeam. (Verses 15, 16, 17) All speak of the mysterious Third One as "She". This refers to the quality of tenderness, sweetness, glorified beauty, with which all are handled when they are under the direct smile of the Mighty One. There is no condemnation to them that walk no longer after the flesh, with its ups and downs, its rights and wrongs, which jerk us so from one estate to another that we are never at peace, never secure, never fearless.

These verses show how like the softness of a beautiful mother's touch is the un-rebuking, un-reproaching Third Presence. Look away unto her and live. Look away unto her and revive. Look away unto her and let the rights and wrongs go on jerking back and forth their determined adherents. So shall the radiance of thy new caught nature cast o'er the scrambling earth its spell of peace. So shall the glory of thy new-caught smile shine on the gloom of earth, and make the prisoners laugh; the street clowns beam with the wisdom that shows how to speak, how to act, how to get safely home. We must expect the impossible, for with him all things wonderful are possible.

Inter-Ocean Newspaper, November 22, 1896

LESSON IX

A Greater Than Solomon

I Kings, 10:1

Balkis, the Queen of Sheba, traveled twenty miles a day for seventy-five days, to see Solomon face to face, and ask him some hard questions. - She stands on the pages of sacred illustrations as the supremest representative of speculative philosophy. She lived four hundred years before Plato, and was as eagerly searching after answers to her sort of questions as he was. Plato never found anybody capable of answering his questions, because they really concerned a different order of truth from what hers did. Balkis wanted to know how to string pearls and perforate diamonds with invisible holes, she wanted to know by what trick of tact or wit Solomon could tell a real wreath of flower from an artificial one, or pick out boys from girls from a group dressed exactly alike.

Plato wanted something different He wanted to know how to subdue the elements of nature; how to converse with the imperishable soul; how to rise superior to famine and death and ignorance. Plato's questions could only be answered by someone whose intelligence struck higher than that occult realm where the thought of the mind can play and lay hold of the stuff that manufactures strong personal magnetisms, strong personal wills, strong personal dominance, strong self-esteem, and quick wit.

No amount of personal magnetism can influence the mighty soul. No amount of strong personal will can force the independent "I Am that I Am" to give down its secret of universal provisions; unkillable universal equal life for all; unerring wisdom for everybody's speech; unalterable kindness in everybody's actions. If Balkis had asked Solomon about how many rights his slaves in the mines under Jerusalem were entitled to, it is not likely that his wisdom had ever ranged along the upper belts where he could have given an answer that would have satisfied an inquirer about the impartial soul. If Balkis had asked him about the noblest kind of prayer a Queen should offer to the all-giving God it is not likely he could have given an answer that would have satisfied one who had discovered that to reign a Queen born in a temporal end earthly realm is wholly ungodly. One who has found that "my kingdom is not of this world" is not asking how a Queen should pray, for she, like Jesus, has declined to be Queen. With all the opportunities, all the accessories, all the good will of multitudes ready to force the young Jesus to accept the throne of the house of David, he was not tempted. He preferred to be wholly identified with the realm where there are no high and low, rich and poor, kings and subjects.

One who identifies himself with Jesus Christ, actually, finds that he is no Balkis-Plato searcher after truth. He discovers that all that Jesus Christ knows and all that Jesus Christ can do is abiding within his own bosom, exactly as Jesus of Nazareth declared: "I make my abode in you," "The Father in me." "All power is given unto me."

All searchers after truth radiate a feeling of hunger like a contagion. One who signs himself in his letters, "Yours, seeking the light," conveys a starving sensation, as poor Goethe crying "More light!" The fact that Jesus of Nazareth could always say, "I am the bread," "I am the truth," "I am the life," "I am," made him a feeder, a supplier. He identified himself with the all-supplying fire in his own bosom. Other men before him had called this flame "the Christ". Others had said it was the saving, redeeming, all-competent God. Others before him had discovered that it hath a still, small voice. Others before him had heard its still, small voice. But who before him had obeyed it?

This lesson is meant to renew an old, old theme, viz., the everlasting presence of the absolutely competent God within our own precincts. Its golden text is: "Behold a greater than Solomon is here". "Here!" Where is "Here"? How near must that greater than Solomon be to us to satisfy us?

Who is satisfied, utterly satisfied, with hearing about wisdom? Who does not hunger to be wise in himself? And that hunger will keep on so long as the stars endure if we do not touch with greater than Solomon here; hear its voice, taste its knowledge, eat its power.

Balkis, who represented speculative philosophy, was so hungry that she was willing to put herself through any amount of Hatha-Yoga, or physical exercise, in order to get a few crumbs. She was jolted on a camel for seventy-five days. She rode through the land of Ishmael, whose intention was to strike everybody he could reach. She carried immense treasures through a tract of robbers on her way. She left the sweet land of "Araby the Blest" to journey through long stretches of dreary wilderness in hopes to find there, at the end, some answers to her puzzling questions.

But the fact was that here, within her own bosom, abode and now abides a greater than Solomon.

When Balkis got the answers to her questions she was greatly, unenviously rejoiced. In that she was like all speculative philosophers. With every new accession of answers to their questions they are as exultant as babies with new rattles. When Plato discovered that the whole visible world is but a colossal system of shadows, imaging some real and unseen world, he was very glad to have caught a bite of so much fact.

And in her willingness to undergo every sort of deprivation in order to get a morsel of fact, Balkis was exactly like all those other half-starved, speculative people we have read of. Diogenes lived in a tub, hoping that cramped quarters would squeeze into sight some grain of truth. Simon4 perched on a tower sixty feet high for thirty years, with his head chained to his ankles, hoping that utter physical discomfort would comfort his mind.

Socrates willingly drank poison that he might deliberately enter the unknown pastures where he had heard there was grass with which to feed hungry creatures like him. Seek, seek, end ye shall find, as Balkis, as Plato, as Simon. But where shall a man seek? This golden text says "here," where each one of us already is, if we would have rest to our soul. He that giveth rest is "here".

The chief note then, of this lesson, is the "here".

The more a man feels this powerful spirit within himself the less hunger he permits around him. Moses drew bread out of the skies. He drew water out of a rock. Somebody communed with the mighty One at Andersonville, and water gushed through the dry sod to quench the prisoners' thirst. Elisha fed a hundred young men with twenty small loaves of barley. The fact is that this One is not scornful like some of our pious religionists declining to consider the common bodily hungers of the masses. It answers questions according to our asking. It feeds according to our requests. But if we deal much with this mighty One we shall get to asking questions of a sort to get mysterious answers. Had Solomon asked of the still small voice about how many wives he ought to keep, how much would he have understood if it had answered as it answered Jesus? "None." "What a long series of questions he would have had to put before it before it could have dawned through his diamond-covered skull that it is given to all humanity to dwell in the kingdom of heaven here and now, and in that kingdom they neither marry or are given in marriage they neither buy nor sell, they never gather into barns to prepare for winter; they never lay up bank stocks for old age.

What a long series of questions even the most enlightened of our age might have to put before we should know whether it is because they in the kingdom of heaven are already eternally united and know that it is settled forever, or whether there is no comradeship heard of in that realm; whether they are never doing anything with their wonderful wisdom in the heavenly land, or whether they are diffusing its glories in never-ending newness.

Many in our age have been told that "the greater than Solomon is here" and have learned to drop their hands and listen to his voice. One man, having heard that each of us corresponds to some number, as taught by Pythagoras, asked, "What is my number?" He had this sentence of Pythagoras' in mind, viz., "Numerals are the invisible coverings of beings, as the body is the visible one." Soon he heard a number. But a woman asked of the still small voice if it was necessary for her to know her number in order to be strong, wise, greater than the trials of human existence. Its answer was "No. I am sufficient for thee."

If Balkis had only heard of this inner voice she might have asked: "Can Solomon answer my questions about pearls and girls?" And it would have answered "Yes." For, indeed, Solomon was equal to these stupendous subjects. But if she had said: "Do I need to travel through the wilderness from Sheba, to Jerusalem for answers to my questions?" It would have answered "No, A greater than Solomon is here." "Here!"

Take notice how many have taught us that we have to travel through wildernesses of pain and trouble, giving all our time, our money, our children, our genius, our words, our writings, our clothes, our gold, our silver, our lands away, leaving home if called, taking the insults of the world if offered, being accused of impossible crimes with silent uncomplaint, to serve truth. How did those mistaken teachers get such horrible misdirections? By asking of the still small voice, "If I forsake everything, suffer everything, can I find truth?" It answered "Yes". But if they had asked, "Is it necessary that I should forsake anything, suffer anything, to know truth?" the answer would have been, as it always has been and ever shall be: "No.

Why have they made the heart of the righteous sad, whom I have not made sad? All my ways are pleasantness and all my paths are peace."

Had Socrates asked, "If I take poison, can I find truth?" It would have answered "Yes". For, "truly, whether covered by flesh or free from flesh, Socrates was bound to find truth. But if he had asked of the still, small voice, do I need to die in order to know truth?" it would have answered "No". There are many in our day who declare that this voice that can answer on every plane a true answer is the voice of our own everlasting "I Am". There are many in our day who declare that this voice that can tell every secret of heaven and earth is the "I Am" of the limitless spaces. Whoever asks, "Are you myself?" its reply is: "Yes", or, "Are you the God of whom the prophets have spoken?" its answer is "Yes." For whether on the prophets' plane or any other plane, that all-indulgent voice is willing to instruct us all as its omnipotent impartiality keeps its answers belonging to that plane. It knoweth that I and my Father are one.

"Do five and three make eight?" asks the young mathematician, and it answers "Yes", but if the Jesus type of mind asks if five and two may be stretched to the capacity of 7,000, he understands its "Yes" when he gets it, and knows how to prove it. Whoever got hold of the message on the door of the Athenian temple, "Know thyself," must have seen in some measure that it is good for us to know what plane we are acting our questions from

before the answers of the indwelling oracle are as
satisfactory as they might be — for the Delphic
temple of Athens, with its oracle inside, was but a
figure of the temple which we are, with our never-
dying oracle abiding within. As great as Solomon
in answering the questions of speculative philosophers, greater than Solomon in announcing to
Jesus that all men alike have indestructible wisdom, power, ability within them.

Solomon never got off the plane of force of either an occult sort or by physical operations.
Balkis was utterly astounded at his exploits on
that plane. She asked him if it was his God that
gave him so many advantages over all other men,
nations, and monarchs of his time; and he told her
that it was his God. She saw that he had struck
the extent of all the truth there is to be had on the
plane of mental and physical force. He truly
thought that there was a deeper set of question-
ings he might put to the deeper God, but did not
put them. So he passed off the stage of human
action not long after the visit of Balkis.

At the time when the greatest thinkers of the
world are praising a man, he is just finding out
that there is a deeper set of questions to a deeper
presence of the inner oracle than that which the
great thinkers are praising him for being so ready
to answer. He must drop his old set and open up
the newer set; else he will get "old," as the next
lesson says that Solomon did. He had stopped with
the old circuit of information as it belonged to one

plane. This step made him stale. A set of deeper questions to a deeper presence would have renewed, refreshed, revived him.

There is no diviner music than Beethoven's and Bach's. It can be taught by asking for it. There is greater power than any that mankind are now showing. It can be taught by asking for it. There is a different way of being instructed from any system of schooling now practiced on earth. It can be had by asking for it. There is a sweeter way of getting bread and raiment than by hiring ourselves out to our neighbors, or hiring them unto ourselves. It can be known by asking for it. Each man, each woman, has so far, asked for guidance and information on that plane where his fathers and mothers landed him, or where his instructors put him. So he and she have had pretty soon to get as stale as the prematurely decayed old

Solomon, who was not yet 60 years of age when he was finished up, because his plane had told him all it had to tell and he declined to go any deeper.

The changeless grandeur of living will eternally be, that we may get deeper and deeper, and as each plane is finished, drink sweeter waters, quaff more inspiring wines, from the same divine Oracle's infinite resources.

"Build thee more stately mansions, oh! my soul,
   As the swift seasons roll.
Leave thy low-vaulted past.
   Let each new temple, nobler than the last,

Shut thee from heaven with a dome more vast,
  Till thou at length art free,
Leaving thine outgrown shell
  By time's unresting sea."

In the heights, the depths, of the unsearched One, whose abode will never cease to be "here," are unused resources for mankind. Ah, blessed by the Lord thy God, which delighteth in the whether thou art seeking his help on the ragman's plane or Solomon's plane. And blessed be thou with his greater gifts, when thou findest that greater than Solomon is he in ability to give and teach.

Solomon made an idol of the plane upon which he lived. Jesus made the "voice" his God. John the revelator "turned to see the voice." It is here. There is no need of hearing any other voice. Listen! "Ask what thou wilt and I will give it thee."

Inter-Ocean Newspaper, November 29, 1896

LESSON X

"Our Destined End Or Way"

I Kings 11:4-13, II Cor. 10:12

A certain man of great age who looked remarkably young was asked how he had preserved his freshness so long. He answered: "By never permitting myself to get either mad or glad." The Bible Lesson for today tells of another man who was always prodding himself up for enjoyment, but was perpetually falling into sorrow. It emphasizes the fact that he was a worn out rag of a man at 45 years of age and a mere piece of dust at 60.

The inference we would glean from hearing about these two men would be that Longfellow was right when he wrote:

"Not enjoyment and not sorrow
Is our destined end or way."

Solomon the subject of our lesson for today, figures on the pages of sacred illustration as a man who swung the pendulum of his own life and the life of a whole nation from madness to gladness, from gladness to madness, during a period of forty years. The nation was supremely glad of its high standing among the nations of the earth; it pointed with pride to its palaces, public roads, fortifications, aqueducts, gardens, reservoirs, but it was as supremely mad against its severe taxations, its forced public labor, its imported idolatries.

So the nation hurried along with Solomon and waxed decrepit about as fast as he did. As a lesson on the physical plane the story of Solomon is meant to warn against making an idol of physical enjoyment. As a lesson on the mental plane the story of Solomon is meant to warn against making an idol of the mind. On both these planes there are "pairs of opposites," or right and left wings; that is, sometimes pleasure; sometimes pain. The mind is very unhappy if it is ignorant or stupid where it had hoped to be informed and shrewd, just as the body is unhappy, if dropped into a fire box where it had hoped to have a downy bed.

We have teachers and preachers on both the physical and mental planes. And on both these planes they are dealing what are the best ways to act with the body in order to keep it happy, and what are the best thoughts to think with a mind in order to make it happy.

The first set of teachers are called physicians. The second set of teachers are called metaphysicians. Solomon, the hero of this lesson, was thoroughly posted in both physics and metaphysics. He knew all the physicians' prescriptions and all the metaphysicians' prescriptions. He declares them both to be vanity. He knew there was another plane which was the real plane, not any vanity about it, but he had got welded into physics and metaphysics so solidly that he would not attend to the real plane. He got such luscious praises for being such a mentally competent man, and such gorgeous honors for being

such a physically competent man, that he dared not risk his head in the halter of the new and untried, lest he become as a crude novitiate and get no more praises.

Last week's lesson explained that his adherence to the two old planes (both vanities) when he knew there was a third plane (not vanity), was what made him stale at 45 years of age. Today's lesson gives in detail the active cause of his physical fading, as well as the active cause of this mental fading. It shows that there was something about him that could not fade. It brings to our attention the fact that there was nothing powerful and self-competent about the God he prayed unto. The getting mad and glad happy and unhappy, by spells to which this man was subject, is never permitted to a man who has once turned his attention to the self-competent God whom Jesus of Nazareth told about.

"The words that I speak unto you, it is not I that speak, but the father that dwelleth in me, he doeth the works."

The regularly accepted commentary on the dealings of the God of Solomon with him reads that his God did everything he could to withstand Solomon's fall. For ages such a kind of pleading being has been preached about as this idol of Solomon. How much we have been told about how essential it is to the activity and helpfulness of the almighty that we have faith in him. People have been continually urged to believe in such a Deity. But Jesus Christ said: "If I do not the works of the father, believe me not."

He said, later on, that He that sitteth on the throne maketh all things new in the sight of all who look his way. He showed that there is a way of beholding Him that sitteth on the throne which changes the world to our sight so that everything looks well, sound, beautiful, happy, wherever we turn. It is not that we purposely change the world's appearance, but its changed appearance is the certain result of beholding Him that sitteth on the throne.

Solomon did not gaze toward such a competent divinity as this. His deity pleaded with him, warned him, threatened him, but never attracted his attention and superintended his conduct.

The Scripture stories describe all kinds of gods, forever softly hinting at the real God. They make Ashtoreth, Milcolm, Molech, and Chemosh to seem more alluring than Solomon's divinity, in order that we may push them all away with their weakling ways and look unto Him that sitteth on the throne of irresistible might, working so independently and effectually that no Solomon can stop him.

This lesson brings up the law of consequences of thoughts and consequences of actions, as if it were a fixed and unalterable performance, in order that we may dive deeper into the mysteries and look higher into the mysteries, and see that there is no consequence of action or thoughts for him that looketh unto Him that worketh great and mighty miracles with us and for us, without asking any of our confidence in Him to help Him along.

No matter what a man had done, it is erased when he turneth to behold Him that is able. No matter what kind of thoughts a man has held they are all erased when he turneth to behold Him that these lessons tell about by their leadings, rather than their wordings. Where are the consequences of bodily actions, where is the fixed laws of effects of thoughts when bodily actions are erased and mind thinkings are blotted out?

Conversation with Him that sitteth on the throne would fill a man's body with divine ability to walk on the waters, to raise the dead out of their graves at the sound of his voice. Conversation with Him that sitteth on the throne would illuminate a man's mind so that he could cause all other men to know their inherited powers and immediately set about using them.

If anybody has visions, voices, emotions, apparitions, or anything else that does not make his eyes, hands, speech, full of new fire, full of new beauty, he has not touched or sighted Him that sitteth on the throne.

He is taking up with Solomon's kind of a god, which Solomon finally changed off for several other gods with more flesh licenses in their commandments.

If we look at these Bible stories without any bias toward any of their gods, we get their straight teachings. Solomon, like Shakespeare, stands out as the giant production of intellect discussing and comparing what the senses feel. They would both lead into the fairy realm of the occult. But whoso looketh unto Him that sitteth on the throne sees that no occult fairy, no occult vision, has any more power than a lie of the tongue or a jealousy of the mind. They are all nothing — nothing at all.

Any god who begs and pleads and warns is not He that sitteth on the throne. Any god who converses with man and does not change that man's body to glow with the beauty it had before it struck this world is not He that sitteth on the throne. It may be the highest god possible to one who describes an incompetent, pleading divinity, but is not the Actual to him that hath no false descriptions.

Aristides conversed with two spirits and was satisfied with their greatness. It was as high as he came. Solomon conversed with a voice that asked for his allegiance and assistance and he was convinced that he was talking with the highest god there was, because he had never claimed any higher kind of deity. Jonathan Edwards had imaginings of a great hand holding men and women in red hot flames, and was certain that he was viewing the maneuvers of all the god there is, because he had never claimed any other kind of deity.

Today's lesson glows with the splendid eloquence of Paul on Mars Hill, and of the voice of the angel of Patmos, with the insistence that we claim an all-working, all-preserving, all-protecting divinity, regarding not our deflections of body or mind, but setting both body and mind into heavenly order according to his own agreement, "I will set all things in order."

It became imperative after a time that Solomon should try Ashteroth, Molech, Chemosh, and Milcom, to see if they had any independent powers of their own, as he had tried his own idol and found him so dependent.

What was his confusion? "Fear God — fear God — fear God." Fearing God, as we all know, means having the eyesight to Him that sitteth on the throne. Did Solomon ever claim the great efficiencies of Him that sitteth on the throne? No.

Why? Because he was biased by his teachers, parents, wives, friends who never claimed an all-competent, independent deity themselves, and therefore, never gave him to feel that he might claim one.

This lesson flames like a smokeless fire with the hot glory of the Truth that men get just the kind of a god they describe, but, if they will stop the clamor of their descriptions, they will find a divine wonder in this universe, who is an independent, competent friend, never asking any assistance, never soliciting any praises, never doing any damage for us to excuse Him for.

This is the new commentary on the life of Solomon which doubtless will shock those who have never known how grand it makes a character to hear even the rustle of the winds moved by Him that sitteth on the throne — the mountain top. Who stoppeth short of the Most High in his attentions shall of course be far from high in his character.

Jesus of Nazareth said; "Sell all thou hast and give to the poor." "The poor ye have with you always." "I am with you always." "I and the Father are one." So sell, let go, the old gods and give your attention to the Poor. Who is that Poor? He is that one who has no needs. Nobody is so free as he who has no needs. The Jesus Christ poverty is having no needs. He that hath no need of our friendship is free. He that hath no need of our faith is free. He that hath no need of us in any way, shape, or fashion is free. Who is then so free as he who clings to nothing and has no needs? Such a wonder is He,

He is the most High One. He is the Throne One. Sell your old gods and see that splendor fall on your life which the unassisted God so easily gives.

Some people are studying up Ashteroth and what sort of a god she was. Some are studying up Molech and his nature. Some are engrossed in Chemosh. Millions upon millions are praying unto Solomon's god, but this lesson about gods and their adherents strikes a deeper chord than its words convey.

Solomon was first biased by his father, then by his prophets, then by his wives. He got so many flatteries from all these people that he dared not sell his biases, but many a time he had an intimation of Him that sitteth on the throne who taketh away the sins of the world, who maketh all things new, who asketh no allegiance or assistance.

As there is reviving youth, beauty, strength in selling off gods, and people's opinions, it is evident that Solomon never sold off his gods or prejudices and biases given him by his contemporaries, for he waxed aged very fast, and died like a cyclone, very suddenly.

The golden text is about standing up in the independence of strength, which the unbiased man receives from the unassisted God. It takes us out of the realm of thoughts. It speaks rather contemptuously of thoughts. It would have us sell even our thoughts — let them go for what they are worth. It tells of a standing upright which is majesty. It tells of it in a rough language. It is found in II Corinthians 10:12. But the Solomon section is I Kings 11:4-13.

The Inter Ocean Newspaper, December 6, 1896

LESSON XI

Solomon's Son

Proverbs 23:15-25

We will consider that Solomon was a great genius and theorist, and a brilliant occultist. That being the case, his theories are true and his occult ozones were the mystical stock out of which he manufactured things that he wanted to use.

The text of this lesson is a quotation from Solomon's wise sayings. It is to be found in Prov. 23:15-25.

When Solomon wrote this chapter 23, he was thinking of the son who was to succeed him on the throne of Israel. He told him things that he himself had been told, but in no particular had ever thought of such a thing as regulating himself by. He urged his son to the utmost regularity and abstemiousness of conduct on the ground of its being dangerous to indulge one's self in bodily pleasure, while yet there was never before him or yet after him one whose indulgence in bodily pleasures was so prodigious and so wearing.

There are some children who do not imitate their parents. They are very few however, especially where they love and enjoy their parents. Rehoboam imitated his father, Solomon, in as many particulars as his wits allowed him leeway. So this chapter on conduct had been used mostly for other men's children, and upon some of them it has had some salutary effect without doubt.

Looking at the descriptions of a religious and abstemious lad which Solomon here gives, we see that he had a good idea and a strong wish that his son might stand up and be an independent character, ignoring the example of his illustrious father.

Looking at the young fellow as a historic object we see that he did not assimilate this metaphysical treatment given him by his father. He did not represent the idea nor fulfill the wish of Solomon. This is on the ground, speaking metaphysically, that everybody around us who is amenable to treatment by us represents our strongest idea on its ascent and on its descent. Everybody who is influenced by us catches our qualities and tendencies more or less.

This is much illustrated by the singular new method of healing now so much practiced by the metaphysicians in the United States. It is the practice of silently causing their neighbors to think as they do. It has been successful in more ways than were advertised, for we have seen how very kindly spirited, large-hearted people have suddenly become prejudiced and uncharitable to keep company with their metaphysical teacher's prejudices and charities.

We have seen how the original minded and independent-spirited teachers have turned out independent pupils while those metaphysical teachers who caught all they knew from somebody else, even while priding themselves on original peregrinations into the high realm of light, have turned out hordes of serviles.

Solomon got his theories from his teachers before him, though he enlarged upon them and brought them out brilliantly as his own. This explains why, on the moral plane, Rehoboam imitated Solomon's example, rather than his precepts.

For Solomon's example was his self-indulgence on every line that pleased him, and having a most splendidly clear idea of excelling everybody else in everything, he self-indulged himself in as superior a fashion as he did everything else. Nobody could come near him in gorgeousness. Rehoboam caught that self-indulgence.

As these lessons are directly applicable to our own times, and each week's text hit our nation's affairs exactly and our own personal affairs exactly, we see from outside, material, external standpoint, just how things are with us by reading about Solomon.

On the outside and external point of rendering the practical application of the texts, his theory of the conduct of life is good, but does not have our heart's staunch support, from the head gun down to the toy pistol of our representative men. From the interior rendering of the text, we are able to strike a chord where the divine tones are more powerful with our life than our heart's staunchest support.

If there were not some deep diapason of possibilities beyond the descriptions, of our great writers, we should certainly have to conclude that human life is a great hoax, demanding our most terrible exertions to keep us from its pitfalls. But there is a deep diapason striking on to it, we find a hand is on the helm of our human life and a voice is inviting our listening ear with only one statement over and over.

W« shall have no seeming friend if we do not see that hand. We shall have no seeming independence of human pitfalls if we do not listen to the voice. But the misfortunes will be only seemings. They will never be substantials. They will never be real. They will never be actual. They will only be veils, the great hand is guiding and the supernatural voice is speaking, and we are all right, whether we seem to be all wrong or not.

This is the diapason; the deeper fact of life. The way to have the real fact shine out is to see the mighty hand, to hear the wonderful voice.

Now the great writers make it out that if we are gluttons, we must struggle not to be gluttons. And if we are fools we must struggle not to be fools. They make us forget as much as they can the wonderful hand on the helm of our life and the enchanting voice in our ear.

Who among them has arisen to sing the new song, the true song, the song celestial, which tells that he who turns to see the hand and hear the voice has not to try and struggle to do rightly, for he sees that he has never really been going any other way but right?

Why, then, is there gluttonous conduct and foolish speech? Only that the young man or old man or woman has never had his or her attention called to the great Omnipotent One, so as to see the actual fact and tear off the veil. The veil is all that seems so bad and hard, and horrifying.

If a child swears and smokes and overeats, call his attention to the mighty hand that is guiding his life into the happy port. Let him see that all that which people say spoils him is not influential on him. He is bound to be right, to be great, to be inspired, whether his actions are agreeable or disagreeable to his acquaintances; but if he once catches sight of the hand on the helm, all that he does will be like the actual life, the great comrade is superintending so well.

There is a divine conduct we are all carrying on. It can come to the surface, and be visible to everybody who sees the one whose hand is on the rudder.

The Solomon whose surface conduct was so reprehensible felt great swells of anguish, as these lessons have often declared, because he kept his eye on the surface conduct and accepted the teachings of his prophets that he was responsible, and must force himself to behave better.

Who of you is a spendthrift or a glutton? Who of you is a beggar, an outcast, or a failure? You are nothing of the kind. In companionship with the divine one, you are now this moment leading a heavenly life in an invincible way. Watch that heavenly one. He is near. Just behind. Just above. Once catch sight of him. Once see how divinely beautiful your path is. That is enough. From the one sight your outer actions show a new nature. Keep watching him. You will like to watch him. He will make you watch. You will see how good your life is. You will admire your own conduct. It will daily show you the protecting hand. You will love the miracles you will see.

There is one more thing about this verse, this hand, this eye, but it is not best to tell about it in this lesson. Perhaps I will never tell it in any written message. No Bible text thus far has brought it well to the front. If they do it in the future - very good, the fact remains that they never yet have.

Taking note of the text of today, we see that some great points, see the sixteenth verse for instance, where Solomon says that if Rehoboam has a wise mind, the Father's heart will have good blood in it, and his kidney will inspire his whole body with new health. The kidneys used to be supposed to be the seat of the deepest and strongest emotions so that it is well known to such metaphysicians as work wisely on the mind plane that emotional people are certain to have kidney complaints.

Solomon wants to have his heart beat better and his kidneys more wholesome and he thinks they would be all right if Rehoboam were not so stupid. He speaks both physically and metaphysically.

The international committee chose the 21st verse of this chapter for the golden text. If anybody studies into the outwardly unpleasant picture made by that verse, he will not be gazing at the great secret beauty of this sweeping life that is really going on all around us. If once they decline to be influenced by such a picture, they will see that the greatest picture of such people is the greatest nothing.

Taking him that abideth near us and guideth continually as the objective point, we choose the last clause of the 17th verse for our golden text, viz.: "Be thou in the fear of the Lord all the day long." "Fear of the Lord" is eye on the Comrade. That Comrade ever near the boy, the girl, the man, the woman. God is his name. Under his hand whoever did go astray? Nobody. Is his hand ever slackened on the child's life? Never. Call the child's attention to Him. He will then look within the veil. He will watch him all the day long.

When a man is in a well trying to climb up and out, he must look up. When he leaves off looking up, he falls. When people warn us of danger, telling us how the angels will weep and wring their little hands if we do thus and so, let us pay no heed to such heart-breaking pictures. Let us watch the Comrade just behind, just above; whose hand is on the rudder of life. Then there will never any harems spread their tinsel walls against the skies of anybody's life! Then there will never any foolish speeches split against the glory of the intelligence belonging to everybody's life! Then there will never any misfortunes shade against the sweet defence of anybody's life! Then there will never any want and pain strike their whipcords against the face of any life.

But though want and pain and harems flourish galore, they are never anything actual. They forever keep on being only veils. The eye that "turned to see the voice" as the Revelator says, shall see how golden, gay is his life forever, how miraculous is his own goodness at every instant. "What I say unto you, I say unto all, watch."

Inter-Ocean Newspaper, December 13, 1896

LESSON XII

Missing

LESSON XIII

Review

Ecclesiastes 12:13

There is but one Bible verse set out as food for our meditation today. It is found in Ecc. 12:13. "Let us bear the conclusion of the whole matters. Fear God and keep his commandments, for this is the whole duty of man."

To fear God is to keep the eye on the Eternal One. To keep his commandments is to be natural. We need not try to live according to the standards arranged for us by our neighbors. If we go on in the perfectly natural way, with the eye of the mind on the Everlasting One, we come to mighty experiences. We come to where we find the majestic influence which is never absent is a willing prompt, sleepless servant.

It was Job who found himself using this most competent servant. "I will command and thou shalt answer. And the Lord was pleased with Job." It was Solomon who became timid before this stupendous menial, and used to listen steadfastly to the roar of the cataract in his garden to keep from realizing that this wondrous domestic was near. Solomon had been trying to fit into standards, that was what made him timid. Job kept himself clear from standards long enough to get a fearless mastery. If it made Napoleon masterful and noble in mien to command a few lean Frenchmen, and makes the English ladies imperious of carriage to control a few Irish housemaids, what shall be the possible manner and indwelling feeling of anyone of us who shall use wise commandments with this splendid servant everywhere present?

David gave an order once, and was astonished to find that a servant had had the order filled before it was given. This is the order, "Show me a token for good that they which hate me may see it." Everything in his realm that opposed him thereafter was in a state of abject awe at the Divine tokens of good that surrounded him. The straight and efficient commandment which David and Moses practiced was what showed that they obeyed with great singleness. That is they watched faithfully. People talk about obeying God, and intimate that the obedience is all on one side. It is time that they knew that he that is greatest among us is the most competent servant we have, and nothing we can do is as obedient to Him as what he can do for us, carrying out our orders. When the lightning gets here, and all out of breath with hurrying so fast, it finds itself ages behind-hand, for the servant has had our tasks finished so long.

Therefore the keeping of a commandment which starts out with being simply natural, finally brings us to be supernatural, for the winds, the seas, the events of nations and all the destinies of Kings are fixed according to our special orders. Truly only a supernatural being can expect to change Kings, and rebound territories with ease. But he that handles a few German troops is nothing by the side of one who handles the Armageddon. The German commander might suffer defeat at the hands of the Czar of Russia or the Queen of England, but he that is accustomed to using Him that is greatest among us need have no fear of failure. The keeping of the commendatory nature within us is a matter of what we command. If we manage our affairs with careful attentiveness our commendatory nature falters with years. If we command our kitchen maids, farm hands, or office boys with noble attentiveness we still notice that the commanding confidence wanes with years. If we manage our writing of books with profoundest, concentration there is the same diminution of commendatory skill. All these lessons finally teach us the necessity of leaning heavily on somebody or something.

The golden text is made the single text for the subject of our meditation this day that we may note a commandment we are privileged to make which has in it an everlastingness to infuse us with. Making it we are charged and recharged with energy, majesty, revivification. Take note again. Is not a man always very like the people he makes use of? Does he not understand them best? Even in driving a tired horse, does not a man feel tired? What, then, might be the effect of driving a tireless, sleepless servant, whose knowledge of all things was unquestionable? What likeness might the face of a man assume or grow into who should use for his daily dromedary an Omnipotent, Omniscient, supernal influence? That is what this text means, pushed to its final interpretation.

When some people read of this golden doctrine they will be shocked. They have heard and practiced the doctrine of being a worm in the presence of God so long that to be a worm is as high as they aspire. They will need to have a certain Bible text repeated to them by somebody.

The text will uplift them from the worm talk and the child talk more quickly than any other in scripture. It teaches that the talk of being a child is as binding to the inspiring meaning of scripture, and keep men as far from seeing his commendatory natures of which this golden text hints, as the determination to be a worm: "Stand thou upright on thy feet, thou worm Jacob. Say no longer, 'I am child.'" "See I have set thee this day over the nations, and over the kingdoms."

Who is the "I" that sets man over nations and over Kingdoms? It is he that is greatest among us, yet who is the servant of all. Giving him orders, what to do enlarges the shoulders and head of a man and straightens him up to his full height.

Note how imperiously David spoke to the one that is greatest among us. Note how firmly Jesus gave his orders. And thus we face David and Jesus as the most royal of men. The book of Ecclesiastes is not a writing of Solomon, but is something that somebody wrote about Solomon. He notes how Solomon gradually ceased to deal directly and authoritatively with the greatest among us; how he got to dealing with his own ideas, with stone images, and finally with pure fear, he sums up a great deal from observing Solomon at his performances. "Fear God," he says. That is, keep no other servant. He is quick enough, competent enough, noble enough for anything.

"This is the whole duty of man," he says. It must be duty enough, then. If, indeed, it takes a good General's whole mind to keep his army in good order, what might it not require of us to keep the army that fills all space informed about what we want done with all the people, all the animals, all the star-loads of living creatures? But chiefest of all, what shall the Almighty servant do for ourselves? Beyond the beauties and strengths of an earthly frame lies the supernal possibility of us all. The Great Servant can fit us up for our wonderful places on that supernal standing ground. If we have supernatural powers there must be supernal places, and events to exercise them upon. Who shall give direction and shape to all these new and wonderful things so well as one who has always served men and angels in those things? They that fear that servant find him prompt and competent.

This text shows how ploddingly men have always been moving about on the globe by reason of never having risen to use the one that is greatest as their servant. It shows how they have been dealing with hypothesis and imaginary premises, and attempting to construct great systems out of nothing, always because of never having used their wonderful servant. Who has ever learned to use the highest postulates and reasonings so that they would work invariably in the way of straightening affairs and conditions? The fact that nobody is reliable in the use of any metaphysical reasonings that have ever been presented shows that they are not half nor a quarter nor a millionth part as good servants as they have been considered to be. Therefore, how silly to fix the single eye on metaphysical reasonings.

Who has ever shown a good, reliable life from following the inner voices or the outer voices that have sometimes set up as oracles in men? Nobody. Therefore, how silly to try to imitate Socrates and Aristides, or any of the modern dopes, with their sick bodies and their bogus voices. Those voices are not worth using as servants. This golden text declares that it is only worth while to single out and use one servant, namely, the one who is greater than armies in number, greater than king's united conclave, greater than angels, principalities, and powers in most devoted effort.

This golden text, however, hints at one movement of man which precedes the commanding use of the mighty servant. It refers to a part of the mystery of the offering up all that we have to the servant before we are as identically one with commanding genius as we have to be in order to use the great One skillfully. Things new and old must be handed up and out with the sweep of the new age shedding its first beams on our earth. It will be seen that the church militant has not been wrong in its doctrines of repentance, conversion, remission, atonement, but through having a misconception of God has used all these servants to no purpose.

The young light breaks through the hills of the foolish doctrines, and the foolish announcements of God, so long looming on the horizon fronting our eyes. It is a new light, a young child. It has new adherents, few friends, few, indeed; who knows about it at all. But the man child, with the sun in the look of his young eyes, is here. All, hail new light, young message, destined to draw the nations up as on cords of irresistible magnetism from pain into peace.

Inter-Ocean Newspaper Dec. 27, 1896

Notes

Other Books by Emma Curtis Hopkins

- *Class Lessons of 1888 (WiseWoman Press)*
- *Bible Interpretations (WiseWoman Press)*
- *Esoteric Philosophy in Spiritual Science (WiseWoman Press)*
- *Genesis Series 1894 (WiseWoman Press)*
- *High Mysticism (WiseWoman Press)*
- *Self Treatments with Radiant I Am (WiseWoman Press)*
- *Gospel Series (WiseWoman Press)*
- *Judgment Series in Spiritual Science (WiseWoman Press)*
- *Drops of Gold (WiseWoman Press)*
- *Resume (WiseWoman Press)*
- *Scientific Christian Mental Practice (DeVorss)*

Books about Emma Curtis Hopkins and her teachings

- *Emma Curtis Hopkins, Forgotten Founder of New Thought –
  Gail Harley*
- *Unveiling Your Hidden Power: Emma Curtis Hopkins' Meta-
  physics for the 21st Century (also as a Workbook and as A
  Guide for Teachers) – Ruth L. Miller*
- *Power to Heal: Easy reading biography for all ages –Ruth
  Miller*

To find more of Emma's work, including some previously unpublished material, log on to:

www.highwatch.org

www.emmacurtishopkins.com

WISEWOMAN PRESS

Vancouver, WA 98665
800.603.3005
www.wisewomanpress.com

Books by Emma Curtis Hopkins

- *Resume*
- *The Gospel Series*
- *Class Lessons of 1888*
- *Self Treatments including Radiant I Am*
- *High Mysticism*
- *Genesis Series 1894*
- *Esoteric Philosophy in Spiritual Science*
- *Drops of Gold Journal*
- *Judgment Series*
- *Bible Interpretations: Series I, thru XXII*

Books by Ruth L. Miller

- *Unveiling Your Hidden Power: Emma Curtis Hopkins' Metaphysics for the 21st Century*
- *Coming into Freedom: Emily Cady's Lessons in Truth for the 21st Century*
- *150 Years of Healing: The Founders and Science of New Thought*
- *Power Beyond Magic: Ernest Holmes Biography*
- *Power to Heal: Emma Curtis Hopkins Biography*
- *The Power of Unity: Charles Fillmore Biography*
- *Power of Thought: Phineas P. Quimby Biography*
- *The Power of Insight: Thomas Troward Biography*
- *The Power of the Self: Ralph Waldo Emerson Biography*
- *Uncommon Prayer*
- *Spiritual Success*
- *Finding the Path*

Books by Ute Maria Cedilla

- *The Mysticism of Emma Curtis Hopkins*
- *Volume 1 Finding the Christ*
- *Volume 2 Ministry: Realizing The Christ One in All*

List of
Bible Interpretation Series

with dates from 1st to 22nd Series.

This list is for the 1st to the 22nd Series. Emma produced twenty eight Series of Bible Interpretations.

She followed the Bible Passages provided by the International Committee of Clerics who produced the Bible Quotations for each year's use in churches all over the world.

Emma used these for her column of Bible Interpretations in both the Christian Science Magazine, at her Seminary and in the Chicago Inter-Ocean Newspaper.

First Series

Second Series

Third Series

Fourth Series

Fifth Series

Sixth Series

September 25 - December 18, 1892

Seventh Series

Eighth Series

April 2 - June 25, 1893

Ninth Series

July 2 - September 27, 1893

Tenth Series

October 1 – December 24, 1893

Eleventh Series

January 1 – March 25, 1894

Lesson 1	The First Adam *Genesis 1:26-31 & 2:1-3*	January 7th
Lesson 2	Adam's Sin and God's Grace *Genesis 3:1-15*	January 14th
Lesson 3	Cain and Abel *Genesis 4:3-13*	January 21st
Lesson 4	God's Covenant With Noah *Genesis 9:8-17*	January 28th
Lesson 5	Beginning of the Hebrew Nation *Genesis 12:1-9*	February 4th
Lesson 6	God's Covenant With Abram *Genesis 17:1-9*	February 11th
Lesson 7	God's Judgment of Sodom *Genesis 18:22-23*	February 18th
Lesson 8	Trial of Abraham's Faith *Genesis 22:1-13*	February 25th
Lesson 9	Selling the Birthright *Genesis 25:27-34*	March 4th
Lesson 10	Jacob at Bethel *Genesis 28:10-22*	March 11th
Lesson 11	Temperance *Proverbs 20:1-7*	March 18th
Lesson 12	Review and Easter *Mark 16:1-8*	March 25th

Twelfth Series

April 1 – June 24, 1894

Lesson 1	Jacob's Prevailing Prayer *Genesis 24:30, 32:9-12*	April 8th
Lesson 2	Discord in Jacob's Family *Genesis 37:1-11*	April 1st
Lesson 3	Joseph Sold into Egypt *Genesis 37:23-36*	April 15th
Lesson 4	Object Lesson in Genesis *Genesis 41:38-48*	April 22nd
Lesson 5	"With Thee is Fullness of Joy" *Genesis 45:1-15*	April 29th
Lesson 6	Change of Heart *Genesis 50:14-26*	May 6th
Lesson 7	Israel in Egypt *Exodus 1:1-14*	May 13th
Lesson 8	The Childhood of Moses *Exodus 2:1-10*	May 20th
Lesson 9	Moses Sent As A Deliverer *Exodus 3:10-20*	May 27th
Lesson 10	The Passover Instituted *Exodus 12:1-14*	June 3rd
Lesson 11	Passage of the Red Sea *Exodus 14:19-29*	June 10th
Lesson 12	The Woes of the Drunkard *Proverbs 23:29-35*	June 17th
Lesson 13	Review	June 24th

Thirteenth Series

Fourteenth Series

Fifteenth Series

Sixteenth Series

April 7-June 30, 1895

153

Seventeenth Series

July 7 – September 29, 1895

Eighteenth Series

Nineteenth Series

January 5 – March 29, 1896

Lesson 1	Missing	January 5th
Lesson 2	Missing	January 12th
Lesson 3	Lesson on Repentance *Luke 3:15-22*	January 19th
Lesson 4	"The Early Ministry of Jesus" *Luke 4:22*	January 26th
Lesson 5	Missing	February 2nd
Lesson 6	Missing	February 9th
Lesson 7	The Secret Note *Luke 6:41-49*	February 16th
Lesson 8	Answered Prayer *Luke 6:41-49*	February 23rd
Lesson 9	Letting Go The Old Self *Luke 9:18-27*	March 1st
Lesson 10	"Me, Imperturbed" *Luke 10:25-37*	March 8th
Lesson 11	Lord's Prayer *Luke 11:1-13*	March 15th
Lesson 12	Be Not Drunk With Wine *Luke 12:37-46*	March 22nd
Lesson 13	The Winds of Living Light *Luke 12:8*	March 29th

Emma Curtis Hopkins was absent on a voyage to Vera Cruz, Mexico to bring her ill son back to the USA. She left December 28, 1895 and returned February 6, 1896. This would account for missing lessons in this quarter. She may have mailed the two in January or they may have been written previously.

Twentieth Series

April 5 – June 28, 1896

Twenty-First Series

July 5 – September 27, 1896

Lesson 1	The Lord Reigneth *II Samuel 2:1-11*	July 5th
Lesson 2	Adeptship *II Samuel 5:1-12*	July 12th
Lesson 3	The Ark *II Samuel 6:1-12*	July 19th
Lesson 4	Purpose of An Adept *II Samuel 7:4-16*	July 26th
Lesson 5	Individual Emancipatioin *II Samuel 9:1-13*	August 2nd
Lesson 6	The Almighty Friend *II Samuel 10:8-19*	August 9th
Lesson 7	Salvation Is Emancipation(missing) *Psalms 32:1-1*	August 16th
Lesson 8	Individual Emancipation *II Samuel 15:1-12*	August 23rd
Lesson 9	Absalom's Defeat And Death *II Samuel 16:9-17*	August 30th
Lesson 10	The Crown Of Effort *I Chronicles 22:6-16*	September 6th
Lesson 11	"Thy Gentleness Hath Made Me Great *II Samuel 22*	September 13th
Lesson 12	A Fool For Christ's Sake *Proverbs 16:7-33*	September 20th
Lesson 13	The Lord is a Strong Tower Proverbs 28:10	September 27th

September 27 of this quarter is a Review of the International Committee listing, not Emma's usual listing and review of the previous lessons in the quarter.

Twenty-Second Series

October 4 – December 27, 1896

CPSIA information can be obtained
at www.ICGtesting.com
Printed in the USA
LVHW08s0621170818
587192LV00026B/578/P